European TARTS

Pastries Like a Pro

Divinely Doable Desserts with Little or No Baking

HELEN S. FLETCHER

Photographs by T. Mike Fletcher

ISBN: 1479127086
ISBN 13: 9781479127085

Helen S. Fletcher, St. Louis, Missouri
European Tarts, Divinely Doable Desserts with Little or No Baking

Dedication

For the two youngest loves of my life – Sam and John for being Sam and John and bringing so much joy into my life.

Top Left, Fresh Fruit Tart, page 37
Top Right, Walnut Lace Tart, page 77
Bottom Left, Triple Chocolate Tart, page 96
Bottom Right, Chocolate Caramel Truffle, Tart, page 50

European Tarts Table of Contents

Foreward

When I first started my bakery, Truffes, Inc, some people warned that pastries made totally from scratch using all butter, 40% cream, the best of chocolate and nuts, with no box mixes, no bucket fillings and icings couldn't possibly make a profit. My belief that quality, consistency and service always sell kept me going in the lean, early years. However, it didn't happen all at once and we were, as many successful businesses, a ten-year "overnight" success.

From a background as a food writer, consultant and traveling teacher, I wanted to find a way to stay in town and do what I did best - bake. Having written articles that appeared in Bon Appétit, Chocolatier and The Pleasures of Cooking as well as authoring my first book, "The New Pastry Cook", I gained some name recognition in St. Louis. With one client to start, I began Truffes, Inc., my upscale, handmade, wholesale pastry business. In the beginning, I started out of my house with a timetable of 6 months to see if I liked baking on a daily basis to the demands of clients instead of for myself, family and friends on an infrequent basis. I had promised my husband I would not turn our home into my place of business. As my clientele grew and I became known for unusual wedding cakes, it soon became clear that I would need to find a commissary from which to work. Because of the sheer cost of equipping a bakery, I set out to find a suitable spot which already had an established food service. This period was probably the most frustrating time in my business life. I looked everywhere and at anything that might work - even if I had to share it. I asked every one I knew, even remotely, if they knew of anywhere and finally a client told me about my location.

Although not equipped as a bakery, but set up for food, we quickly got rid of deep fat fryers and steam tables, and added ovens, refrigeration, a freezer and a 12 quart and 20 quart mixer in addition to my 5 quart mixer from home. When I was working out of my house, I stored all of my equipment in my son's former bedroom. After seeing the shelves of equipment one day, he exclaimed in dismay that I had turned his room into a "warehouse". All of this equipment was moved into my 800 square foot commissary. I was on my way and I couldn't decide in the beginning whether I was excited and happy or just plain scared to death. It changed from minute to minute as I saw, in very short order, just how much I had to learn - and quickly!

In the beginning, everything was made to order. The client would call on a Monday or Tuesday and we would deliver on Thursday or Friday. With enough business to keep me busy 3 days a week doing the baking and finishing, pan washing and cleaning, it became evident that more clients were needed. So I added salesman to my growing list of newly developing talents. The first three years were such a steep learning curve, I almost fell off more than once. When I first started the business, I sold what I wanted to make. However, it didn't take long for me to listen to my clients to learn what they wanted. In the beginning I didn't make a carrot cake, not because they aren't good, but my line was more European and I felt it didn't really fit in.

It took me a while to catch on and decide if I were going to make a carrot cake, as it appeared I had to, it would have to be the best one around. I learned, but sometimes it took me longer than it should have. However, my saving grace was I started learning faster and faster as the company grew at a rapid pace.

I soon hired my first dishwasher for 3 days a week and thought I was living mighty high.

I continued to add part time help to make Press-In crusts for the tarts, chop chocolate, squeeze lemons and do some of the other more time consuming chores. Soon, full time help was needed, more space was required, and the line was turned from made to order to frozen, in order to keep up with our competition. The product line was culled and anything that did not thaw and retain its quality was eliminated. I did regular assessments of my competition and it became apparent we could not sustain growth as a made to order business. Especially, since it became obvious that our main competition was large distributors that brought in frozen desserts from out of town. In addition to a much more stable product with a longer shelf life, the distributors could offer next day delivery, which I couldn't. To solve that problem we took over the adjacent 800 square foot bay, broke through the wall and added, what we thought at the time to be a monstrous combination refrigerator/freezer. The plan worked better than expected and within a few months we were crowding our freezer something fierce. Fifteen months later we took another bay, opened another door, added another freezer, a cutting machine and a packaging machine to ease our labor problems as well as equipped the bakery with more ovens, and larger mixers. With 2400 square feet and approximately 100 clients, our biggest problem was to wean our wonderful clients away from their favorites and let us add new items. They always wanted the new but hated to give up anything old. With about 100 items offered, it was difficult sometimes to keep up. But quality and consistency whether in product or service remained our guide and we went to great lengths to be of help.

The most important thing I have learned is that anyone, with or without specialized training, (I have had no training) but a keen interest in a subject, can master that subject if they just remember to enjoy it as they go. Almost all of my employees, had little to no baking experience, but they learned to produce all the items in this book and a great deal more. To say I have not experienced great frustration would be to misrepresent reality. However, learning to work with people, being able to help my clients, learning so much of the nitty-gritty of running a successful business has given me more pleasure than I fear I have returned. And even on my worse day, I still loved it!

Introduction

In the Beginning

Left, Rum Raisin Tart, page 94
Right, Honey Almond Tart, page 70

European Tarts Introduction

The uniqueness of this book lies in the fact that all of these tarts were made in my bakery, Truffes, Inc. in St. Louis, Missouri for more than 23 years and sold wholesale to restaurants, caterers and hotels. Although they were produced in quantity at the bakery, each recipe and their component parts have been tested and re-tested for a single recipe made in a home kitchen for this book. There are many factors that are different when baking for production and baking at home. Key among them are ovens used, various mixer sizes (we had five different sized mixers that could accommodate bowls from 5 quarts to 80 quarts) as well as ingredients not available to consumers. While this book uses seedless red raspberry jam, at the bakery we used a product called European Raspberry Filling from Henry and Henry. It was bake proof, meaning it would not turn liquid when baked and it had more body for piping, making it much easier to use than jam, which loses its body when whisked for piping. However, I have fortified the jam used in this book so it works fine and there is no difference in taste. Emulsified powdered sugar is another example. We could sprinkle items with emulsified powdered sugar and it would not liquefy in the refrigerator or on thawing as will normal powdered sugar. At home, sprinkling with powdered sugar when ready to serve solves this problem.

At the shop, we made large amounts of lemon curd, pastry cream, press-in crusts, buttercream and cream glaze among other things so they would be readily available when we needed them. We never knew when an order for 500 to 1500 pieces of a single dessert would be ordered. Having stock items available meant we didn't have to turn down orders because short notice.

One of the advantages of these recipes, is the majority of them can be made and frozen which is how we sold them to our customers. Caterers and hotels want frozen desserts because they are much easier to cut and plate than thawed desserts. They are plated on site, put on huge racks, covered and held either in a cooler (refrigerator) or at room temperature. If the item was to be thawed first, as in the case of restaurants, we specified to thaw them in their boxes to avoid condensation on the top of the tarts. By thawing in the boxes, the condensation, which naturally forms, goes to the top of the box, not the top of the tart. I could always tell if our suggestion was adhered to by looking at the thawed product. In the case of these tarts made at home, it is best to thaw them in the refrigerator the day before use, covered, if possible. Foil may be used to cover them if used loosely.

This is the ideal book with which to start baking. Made in 9x3/4 inch or 11x 3/4 inch deep quiche pans with removable bottoms, twenty-one of the twenty-seven tarts require no baking other than the crust. With a few exceptions, the crusts are either a graham cracker type crust or a cookie dough crust that are pressed into the pans. European tarts, as I use the term, refers to a short profile pastry, usually not more than one and one half inches tall. They are beautifully finished and the taste belies their ease of preparation. While short in stature, these tarts are rich and intense in flavor. Although some of the finishes may look difficult to a novice, all are very easy to execute with just a little practice. This is definitely a confidence building book. Each of the recipes found in this book were used in my bakery and, as such, have been tested and retested over the years. In addition to the full sized tarts, individual tartlets may be made using 3 1/2 to 4 3/4 inch tartlet shells. The 11 inch tarts will make 9 to 10 individuals and the 9 inch tarts make 7 to 8 individual tartlets. Simply divide the recipes by the number of tartlets, fill and finish as directed for the full sized tarts.

While professional bakers and pastry chefs always use scales to weigh ingredients as opposed to using measuring cups for volume, I have included cups, grams and ounces so anyone can use and follow the recipes although I strongly recommend weighing for accuracy and speed.

Each chapter includes general notes applying to all of the recipes in that chapter. It is most helpful to read these notes before embarking on a recipe.

These recipes are the basis for your own imagination. Mix and match or use one or more components to enhance your own ideas.

Because there were too many photographs to include in this book, there is an accompanying blog; www.europeantarts.com that consists of how-to photographs as an additional assist.

About The Photography

Not so candid photography

About The Photography

T. Mike Fletcher's photographic career has taken him all over the world with assignments for editorial, advertising, corporate and political photography for decades. He entered the world of food photography to illustrate his wife's first book, "The New Pastry Cook" and has collaborated with her ever since.

A finished picture of most of the tarts is featured within the book to give you a reference to what the finished tart should look like.

Because it is impossible to include as many how-to photographs as I would like within the book, a companion blog, www.europeantarts.com has been set up to reference these. Look in the search box or the index. I have cross-indexed photos and items to make things as easy as possible.

The number of how-to photos varies and depends upon what is important in that particular tart. For instance, the procedure for making a glaze or truffle filling is the same no matter what the ingredients, so that procedure is shown once. The same goes for the crusts. Lemon curd is featured but the procedure is the same for all the other curds.

Culinary Terms

Have you ever wondered
what the difference
is between beating
and whisking?

Culinary Terms

This is a listing of baking terms as used in this book.

Add refers to putting or mixing another ingredient into a recipe.

Beat refers to vigorously mixing ingredients together either by hand or with a mixer as the recipe directs. According to "Food Lovers Companion", "110 hand strokes equals 1 minute of beating with a mixer." Personally I'm not going to challenge that!

Bake. To cook in an oven with dry heat. It is important to check an oven frequently with an oven thermometer as an oven can bake hot or cold in which case the temperature must be lowered or increased accordingly by that amount. A clean oven is essential to even baking. One way to help keep an oven clean is to line the bottom with foil, making sure vent if openings are cut out if using a gas oven. It is simple to remove the foil and replace it with new. As ovens age, they tend to develop hot spots which will brown faster. Turning the pan in the oven so the opposite, less browned side is to the hot spot can even out the baking.

Basket weave is a design used to finish pastries. It generally uses a special #47 or #48 basket weave pastry tip. It is made by piping rows about 1/2 inch apart across the tart. Turn the tart one-quarter turn and pipe another row in the same manner and lastly, repeat one more time. The edge is finished with a decorative finish. *The Chocolate Caramel Truffle Tart is an example.*

Beat until stiff. Meringue and whipped cream are often directed to beat until stiff. A mixer is usually used for this task and it is fitted with the whisk attachment. The ingredients are beaten slowly at first, and then moved up increasingly to high. There are several stages to beating these products. Chantilly stage is reached when the cream just begins to thicken but doesn't hold a peak. The soft peak stage is reached when the whisk is withdrawn and the peaks droop over but do not stand straight up. Medium peaks refer to peaks that barely hold a peak straight up without drooping. Stiff peaks are very firm and stand straight up when the beater is withdrawn.

Blanch. To blanch or blanching refers to immersing a fruit or vegetable in boiling water briefly and then plunging them into cold water to stop the cooking. It is used to loosen skins for removal, set the color of vegetables (think green beans, broccoli) and flavor before freezing. Blanching also refers to plunging nuts into boiling water to remove their skins.

Blanks are the term used to describe a product that is partially finished such as a tart that is filled with pastry cream. It can be refrigerated or frozen until it is needed. If frozen, it is thawed and finished with fresh fruit on top or used in any manner desired.

Blend refers to combining two are more ingredients together using a spoon, mixer or beater. This is usually done on low to medium speed with a mixer and paddle attachment, as it is undesirable to beat in a lot of air.

Blind Baking a Shell refers to the shell being baked without a filling. Depending upon the type of crust, the shell is lined with foil and filled with beans to keep it in place and prevent it from shrinking or falling down when baking. About 2/3 of the way through baking the foil and beans are removed and the shell is put back in the oven to finish baking. When cooled, it can be used for any number of unbaked fillings.

Boil refers to heated water that vigorously bubbles and reaches a sea level temperature of 212 degrees.

Chevron refers to a line in the shape of a V. As a decoration in pastry, it is made by piping lines across a pastry and then, with a toothpick or bamboo skewer, lightly draw a line straight down through the piping. At the bottom, move over the desired width and draw a line straight up. Continue across the product. So it is a down and up motion that produces the V. *The Lemon Raspberry Tart is an example.*

Cover Directly refers to plastic film being placed directly on top of the item not over the bowl. There should be no air bubbles between the item and the film. This prevents the top from getting a skin on top and keeps it from drying or cracking.

Cream. This has two meanings. 1. Cream is the milk fat that rises to the top of milk after it sits. It comes in various forms, depending upon the amount of milk fat it contains. Coffee cream, half and half (consisting of half milk and half cream), whipping cream which is 36% fat and 40% or heavy cream that is 40% fat are among the most common products available to consumers. 2.**To cream** refers to beating an ingredient or several ingredients (most notably in baking, butter and sugar) until soft, lightened in color, increased in volume and homogeneous.

Crush. To pulverize by reducing food to its smallest form as in crumbs, paste or powder.

A mortar and pestle, rolling pin or food processor are some of the tools used to accomplish this.

Curd. As used in this book curds refers to a preserve with a thick consistency made from fruit, butter, eggs, and sugar. *See the Curd Chapter.*

Cutting - To professionally cut the tarts, you need a tall container large enough that a bread knife can fit into. Fill it with the hottest tap water available. Have several paper towels next to the container. After releasing the tart, dip the knife in the hot water to heat it and quickly wipe it dry. Immediately, make the first cut. If the tart is chocolate, let the knife melt the chocolate slightly before cutting straight down. Slide the knife out of the tart at the bottom. Do not bring the knife up to the top. Reheat and re-wipe the knife for every cut.

European Tarts is the name I gave to a classification of tarts in our bakery line. They were made in shallow quiche pans of various sizes and could be sweet or savory.

Fold. The purpose of folding is to combine a light, usually aerated mixture with a heavier mixture. The lighter mixture is poured on top of the heavier mixture, sometimes with flour or another ingredient to be folded in. A rubber spatula is plunged into the center of the bowl all the way to the bottom. The spatula is moved across the bottom of the bowl and up the nearest side, turning the mixture over so the heavier mixture is to top. The bowl is turned about an eighth of a turn while continuing the folding motion. It is important to fold gently as well as quickly with as few strokes as possible to keep the mixture from losing air which is often the only leavening agent used (as in sponge).

Frangipane is of French derivation and is used as a filling in pastries. It uses almonds and sometimes crème patisserie.

Glaze is a thin, shiny coating for either cold or hot foods, which are poured on in a liquid, state and allowed to set up.

Lattice is a finish used on pastry where strips of dough are overlapped so that the product underneath shows through. *The Cranberry Linzer Tart is an example.*

Liquefy. To make an ingredient liquid by processing, blending or heating.

Mix refers to stirring together lightly by hand or with a mixer, usually a few items that are to be added to another mixture.

Off Heat is exactly what it says. Take the pan off the heat before proceeding.

Partially baked refers to baking a crust or other item only incompletely. It is then filled or topped and put back into the oven to finish baking. This technique is used when the filling or topping will be in the oven only a short time, which will not allow the crust to bake through.

Pastry Cream is the English name for the French crème patisserie that is used for filling many pastries or as an ingredient in other fillings. It consists of milk, eggs, sugar, vanilla (or other flavorings), and a thickener such as cornstarch, flour and/or gelatin. *See the Pastry Cream chapter.*

Press-in Crusts are tart crusts that require no rolling out. A portion of the crust is pressed against the side of the pan with the remainder pressed onto the bottom. *See the Crust Chapter.*

Pricking refers to a fork or a tool called a docker making small holes in dough; particularly the bottom of crusts to keep them from rising or bubbling up when baked blind.

Process or processing._As used in this book, refers to the act of using a food processor.

Puree. Any food that is finely mashed to a smooth consistency. The food, usually fruit or vegetables, is cooked first then put in a processor or blender or forced through a sieve.

Release. To release an item refers to getting it out of its container. There are several ways depending upon what you are releasing. Often the item is refrigerated to firm up and the edges are heated with a blowtorch or heat gun at which point it will slide down. For the short quiche pans used in this book, a pointed offset spatula is most helpful by inserting it between the pan and the crust. It usually suffices to do this every 5 or six scallops and is not necessary on every crust.

Shell is another name for a container that holds food such as a crust, chocolate or candy shell. It can also refer to the outer coating of a nut.

Simmer refers to the temperature a liquid that reaches a temperature of 180 degrees. It has small bubbles around the edge of the container or breaking the surface.

Sprinkle. To lightly shower a surface or an item with flour, powdered sugar or another ingredient.

Steam, to. Steaming preserves the shape and texture of many foods because it is a more gentle way of cooking than boiling or poaching directly in water. A rack is placed in a pan with simmering water on which a bowl or pan can be placed with the food in it. The rack must be high enough to keep the pan with the food out of the water. The larger pan is covered with a lid to allow the steam to cook the food. A steamer basket can also be used. It has feet on it to keep the food out of the water. *See the Chocolate Truffle Tarts with Candied Cranberries.*

Stir. To move ingredients around a bowl or pan using a spoon or other utensil.

Tart as used here refers to a shallow pastry that is filled. It can be baked or unbaked. It is made in a tin with fluted sides and a removable bottom and can be made in a variety of sizes.

Toast, to. As used in this book, refers to browning nuts or coconut in an oven. Toasting brings out the flavor. If the nuts are to be ground, make sure they are completely cooled first if using a processor or they can easily turn into a paste.

Toss, to. Refers to very lightly mixing ingredients by tossing them with a fork so they don't compact.

Very Hot refers to liquid that is heated to just below the simmering point or about 175 degrees.

Whipped Cream. Whipping cream with 36% milk fat or 40% or heavy cream with 40% milk fat is beaten with a whisk in a mixer (usually) to trap air and expand in volume. Powdered sugar and vanilla or other flavorings can be added. It can go through several stages from chantilly, which is just thickened to very firm, which can be piped or used to frost a cake. We whipped 40% cream to finish several of our cakes as it has a higher fat content that makes it hold up much better. We also froze them. Other than the powdered sugar and vanilla, no stabilizers were ever added. The cakes thawed with no harm to the whipped cream frosting.

Whisk. To whisk or whisking refers to a specific tool (*see Equipment Section*) that mixes ingredients more thoroughly than a spoon or fork. It can also be used to whip cream by hand and remove lumps from dry ingredients.

Ingredients

What you need for
what you want to do

Ingredients

This compendium relates to the ingredients used in this book.

Almond Extract is a flavoring made by combining bitter almond oil with ethyl alcohol. Extracts are very concentrated flavoring agents that are usually made through evaporation or distillation. The value of extracts lies in the intense flavor that can be added without altering the consistency or adding volume to the product.

Almond Paste is made with ground almonds, sugar and glycerin or other liquid and can be flavored with almond extract. It should not be confused with marzipan, which is similar but sweeter and bound with egg whites. It is used in decorations and can be rolled out and applied to cakes just as fondant is used. Almond paste is used as an ingredient whereas marzipan is a final product.

Amaretto is an almond flavored liqueur. It originally came from Saronno, Italy.

Apricots, dried. Dried apricots are used here to produce lekvar, which is an intense apricot filling of Hungarian origin. When reconstituting the apricots do not cover the pan as most dried apricots are treated with sulfur to help retain their color. By leaving the pan uncovered, the taste of sulfur is erased.

Baking Powder is a leavener consisting of baking soda, an acid such as cream of tartar and a moisture-absorbing ingredient such as cornstarch. When mixed with liquid carbon dioxide gas is released causing the product to rise. There are two type of baking powder. **Single acting baking powder** releases its gas as soon as moisture is introduced. **Double acting baking powder** releases part of its gas when moisture is introduced and the remainder when heat is applied. Double acting baking powder is the most commonly used and is readily found on supermarket shelves. It should be kept in a cool, dry place, as it is perishable. To test the powder, combine 1 teaspoon with 1/3 cup hot water. It should bubble vigorously if it is good.

Brandy is liquor distilled from wine or fermented fruit juice. Aging in wood contributes to the flavor and color.

Butter is made by churning cream until it separates into a semisolid and a liquid known as curds (solids) and whey (liquid). If you care to experiment, butter can be made at home by whipping 40% or heavy cream until it turns to butter. I was renowned at one position I held for having turned 16 quarts of cream into butter by simply about forgetting it while it was whipping. It became known as "Helen's Butter". The good news was, we used every bit of it! On August 31, 1989 the United States Department of Agriculture (USDA) established standards for grades of butter based on flavor, body, texture, color and salt (if present). Butter must be at least 80 percent milk fat with the remaining 20 percent water and milk solids. The grades are based on a score of 100 with AA being the finest at 93, A at 92 and B at 90. AA and A are the most commonly available. Butter may be colored with annatto and can be salted or unsalted, which is often referred to as sweet butter as opposed to salted butter. Salt is used as a preservative. Salted butter will stay fresher longer than unsalted butter. If buying unsalted butter in large amounts it is safer to freeze it if it is not being used within two weeks to preserve its flavor. Butter absorbs flavors around it so it should be stored tightly wrapped. The recipes in this book use only unsalted butter. There are also butters from Europe that have a higher milk fat percentage. All recipes in this book are based on US butter. **Brown Butter** is used as a flavoring agent. It is made by heating butter until it comes to a boil. Reduce the heat to a simmer and cook it until the milk solids, which will drop to the bottom of the pan, turn a golden brown. Care must be taken as the solids go from golden to burned quickly.

Chocolate comes from a tropical cocoa bean. The beans are removed from their pods, fermented, dried, roasted and cracked to remove the nibs. Grinding the nibs to remove some of the cocoa butter leaves a thick, dark paste called chocolate liquor that will undergo further refining. If additional cocoa butter is removed and the remainder is ground, it becomes cocoa powder. At this point, additional ingredients such as sugar or milk may be added and the chocolate will be further refined. Before the chocolate is packaged for sale, it is conched for 12 to 72 hours. Conching consists of rotating blades slowly blending the heated chocolate to remove additional moisture and volatile acids. Chocolate is marketed as **unsweetened, bittersweet, semisweet, sweet and milk chocolate containing at least 12 percent milk solids** (in the form of dry milk) **and 10 percent chocolate liquor.** Companies usually offer more than one kind in any of these categories. **White chocolate** is not actually chocolate. It is a blend of cocoa butter, sugar, milk solids, lecithin and vanilla or vanillin. It is important to read the label and if it doesn't contain cocoa butter it is confectionary coating or summer coating which doesn't melt as does white chocolate. In recent years, the percentage of cocoa solids has been creeping upward with 85% being the current high. This produces an intensely chocolaty chocolate, which is very smooth.

When liquefying chocolate, it is important to keep if from getting too hot and to keep any moisture from reaching it as the chocolate can seize which simply means gum up with no apparent way of getting it smooth. If this happens, you can add a little vegetable shortening or cocoa butter a little at a time to get it back to a liquid consistency. Although I have seen chocolate being melted in the microwave at full power, I prefer the safer method of melting it at 50% power. It can also be melted in a double boiler over barely simmering water. When adding liquid to chocolate add 1/4 cup or more liquid to 6 ounces or less chocolate to prevent seizing.

Cinnamon is a widely used spice in cooking and baking both sweet and savory. It comes in cinnamon sticks also called quills, ground to a powder form and oil. The quills are used whole to flavor a liquid and the powdered form is used in every form of cooking and baking including sweet and savory. Cinnamon is the inner bark of a tropical evergreen tree. There are a number of species sold as cinnamon. Ceylon (Sri Lanka) is considered the true cinnamon dating back to Chinese writings from 2800 B.C. It is considered less sweet with a more complex, citrus flavor. There is Korintje cinnamon that is Indonesian with a smooth flavor and less bite. It comes from the southwest coast of Sumatra where it grows wild on government-protected slopes of Mount Kerinci. Vietnamese cinnamon and Cassia or Chinese cinnamon are native to Southeast Asia, especially southern China and Northern Vietnam. It has a strong, spicy-sweet flavor that is sold in supermarkets.

Cocoa Powder. Powdered, unsweetened chocolate liqueur. **Dutch cocoa** has been treated with an alkali to help neutralize chocolates natural acidity. It is considered milder than regular cocoa powder that has a more assertive taste. Either one may be used in this book.

Cocoa Butter is a cream colored vegetable fat which is the by-product of making chocolate and cocoa powder.

Coconut as used in this book refers to packaged shredded, sweetened coconut. It can be used as it comes or toasted, as the recipe calls for.

Coconut Macaroon Cookies are sold in supermarkets and are used for a crust. They are firm, crispy and are flavored with coconut.

Cornstarch is a powder obtained from the endosperm of the corn kernel. It can be used as a thickener as well as an anti-clumping agent as in powdered sugar.

Cornsyrup made by mixing cornstarch with acids or enzymes, is thick, sweet syrup. It comes in light, which is clear, and dark which is almost black and has a distinct flavor. It deters sugar crystallization when added to sugar syrups.

Cream is the byproduct of unhomogenized milk that, upon standing, separates into two layers, a rich cream on top and skim milk on the bottom. While there are many varieties of cream, the one used in this book is heavy cream or 40% cream. It is used in this book both whipped and unwhipped. **Half and Half** is a mixture of equal parts of milk and cream with 10 to 12 percent fat.

Cream Cheese is an original American cheese developed in 1872 from cow's milk. Its spreadable consistency makes it popular in both savory cooking and sweet baking. By law, it must contain a minimum of 33 percent butterfat and not more than 55 percent moisture.

Neufchatel cheese is the lower version with 23 percent butterfat and less moisture. Lower fat cream cheese can be substituted in most recipes unless otherwise stated.

Cream of Coconut is made from coconut paste, water and sugar. It often separates in the can and should be whisked to bring it together before using. Do not confuse this with coconut milk, which is a different product and can't be substituted.

Dark Rum (see rum)

Eggs as used in baking come from hens and are graded and sized by the USDA. Eggs are graded AA, A, B and C in descending order with the classification being determined by both exterior and interior qualities with the freshness of the egg the main criteria. Exterior quality is determined by shape, texture, soundness and cleanliness. Interior quality is determined by the size of the air cell between the white and shell at the large end of the egg (the smaller the size of the air cell, the higher the quality and freshness of the egg). Also important is the portion and density of the white and the firmness and defects of the yolk. In fresh eggs both the white and the yolk stand high when cracked. Eggs are sold by the weight of a dozen eggs. Each egg does not necessarily weigh the same but they must total the given amount for the specified size. Jumbo size is 30 ounces, extra large is 27 ounces, large is 24 ounces, medium is 21 ounces, small is 18 ounces and pee wee is 15 ounces per dozen. Large eggs are the most used in baking and the eggs specified in this book. The exterior color of the egg has nothing to do with the quality or taste.

Emulsified. Any one of a number of mixtures that normally cannot come together on their own. Think of mayonnaise, which consists of oil, egg yolks and vinegar or lemon juice. By slowly adding the oil to the egg yolks and vinegar or lemon juice and whisking vigorously, a thick satiny emulsion is achieved. Emulsified powdered sugar has been treated in such a way as to prevent it from liquefying or becoming watery in a refrigerator or upon defrosting if frozen. It is generally sold to bakeries only.

Flour. All purpose flour and **cake flour** are the two flours used in this book. Although many grains can be made into flour, as used in this book, both the all purpose and cake flour come from wheat. They are sometimes combined to make pastry flour, which is not readily available to consumers. We used this method at the bakery so we wouldn't have to stock another flour. By combining two-thirds all-purpose flour with one-third cake flour the gluten content is lowered and is close enough to use wherever pastry flour is called for. The strength of flour is determined by the gluten or protein count of that particular flour. The higher the protein count, the stronger the flour. Strong flours are used for blending with other flours and for bread. Soft flours are used for pastries, cakes and biscuits among other things. Pastry flour falls in between and is used for tart shells as well as other items. All-purpose flour is between 9 to 12 percent protein. Cake flour is between 5 to 8 percent protein and the softest of flours. Weights of the flours depend upon whether they are sifted or unsifted. ***Please see the weight chart for more information.*** All-purpose flour comes bleached or unbleached and can be used interchangeably. Flour can be bleached either by aging it or using chemicals. While most flours on the market are presifted, how they are measured can make a huge difference to the outcome. The only sure way of obtaining the correct measure is to weigh the flour, which is why scales are used professionally and highly recommended for home baking. In addition to being more accurate, it is much faster. While the flours are sifted at the point of origin, shipping and stacking can condense them. So if a scale is not being used, stir the flour with a spoon in the bag or canister, dip the cup in and fill to overflowing, then sweep the excess off with the back of a knife. If a recipe calls for sifted flour, place an empty cup measure on a piece of waxed paper and fill a sifter or strainer about half way with four and sift into the cup to overflowing. Sweep the excess off with the back of a knife. This should yield the closest measure to a cup of flour that has been weighed. All recipes in this book use flour that has been weighed.

Food coloring comes in liquid, gel and powdered form. It is used, as it's name implies to color food products.

Fruits used in this book consist of **blueberries, cranberries, lemons, limes, oranges, peaches, pears, raspberries and strawberries** that are fresh or sometimes frozen.

Fruit jams and preserves. Jams consist of fruit and sugar cooked until the fruit is so soft it is formless. Jams are usually purees. They are sometimes set with pectin. **Preserves** are fruit and sugar cooked, sometimes with pectin but the fruit is left in large to medium size pieces. Both are used in pastries. The preserves are often pureed in a processor for a smoother filling.

Gelatin is an odorless, tasteless and colorless thickening agent that forms a gel when ultimately combined with a hot liquid. Gelatin is a collagen, a naturally occurring protein

produced from the bones, tendons and cartilage of various animals. Most of the commercial gelatin is made from pigskin. As the Muslim and Jewish religions forbid the use of pork products, there are other gelling agents available for special diets including vegetarian.

Gelatin comes in a granular form of different strengths, measured by bloom that must be softened in water before adding to a liquid. If the liquid is hot, the softened gelatin can be added without liquefying it first. If the liquid is cold, it must be heated before adding it to the other ingredients. Gelatin sheets or gelatin leaf in paper-thin sheets come in various strengths. They are soaked in water before adding to the product. The colors refer to the strength of the gelatin: Bronze is 125 to 155 bloom, Silver is 130 bloom, Gold is 190 to 220 bloom and Platinum is 235 to 265 bloom. I used powdered gelatin 250 bloom strength. Knox gelatin sold in grocery stores is fine for small amounts. Each envelope contains 2 1/2 teaspoons, enough to jell 2 cups of liquid or 1 1/2 cups of solids. It must always be softened or "bloomed" in cold water, then added to a hot mixture directly or heated to a liquid if the mixture it is being added to is cold.

Graham Cracker Crumbs are made from crushed graham crackers that are a rectangular shaped cracker made from whole-wheat flour. They are used in this book in tart crusts. Graham Cracker crumbs are widely available in grocery stores but whole graham crackers can be crushed if necessary.

Honey is derived from the nectar of flowers gathered by bees as a source of food for them when it is cold or they are unable to get fresh food. It is thick, sweet and sticky and is stored in honeycombs. Generally, the darker the color, the more intense the flavor. There are hundreds of kinds of honey flavored by the nectar from various flowers such as lavender, wildflower and the most common in America, clover honey, orange blossom and sage. It is sold in honeycomb form, with chunks of the honeycomb in with the honey and liquid honey that has been extracted from the comb. It should be stored in a cool, dry place. If it crystallizes it can be reconstituted by microwaving for 30 to 40 seconds at full power, depending upon the amount or by placing the container in a pan of simmering water. Honey is used in both sweet and savory preparations and makes a delicious spread for toast when mixed with butter.

Instant coffee is used as a flavoring agent or to deepen the flavor of chocolate. It is made from heat dried fresh coffee and must first be dissolved in liquid before adding to other ingredients. Instant espresso is generally too strong and should not be substituted.

Mascarpone Cheese comes from the Lombardy region of Italy. It is a double cream or can be a triple cream cheese that ranges from very soft to room temperature butter. Its richness is most known in the United States as the main ingredient in tiramasu. Although it is sometimes suggested that cream cheese be substituted mascarpone, it is not a substitution I recommend since cream cheese is nowhere near the consistency or flavor of mascarpone.

Nuts are used throughout this book both as the star and in supportive roles. The nuts used are **almonds, macadamias and walnuts. Peanuts**, thought of as a nut, are actually legumes. Nuts benefit from toasting to amplify their flavor.

Peanut Butter is made by crushing peanuts into a smooth paste. It had been used by centuries in various forms since George Washington Carver started the peanut butter craze in America, although that was not his intention. He originally used it to feed hungry children in the south and to provide them with protein in an easy to eat, inexpensive form. From there it became, and still is, one of the most popular foods in America. It was promoted as a health food at the 1904 World's Fair. Most of us never outgrow our love of peanut butter. Peanut butter, as most of us know it, comes in smooth and chunky and is often enhanced with sugar and/or other sweeteners, vegetable oils and salt. Natural peanut butter is made with few or no additives and substituting this for the above will alter the final products in this book.

Pectin is a natural, water-soluble substance used for thickening jams, jellies and preserves. It is present in various ripe fruits and vegetables with apple pectin being among the most used. It is added to fruits that lack enough natural pectin on their own to thicken. It's available in liquid form, and powder from citrus fruits or apples. To be effective, the correct balance of sugar and acid must be available in the recipe.

Raisins are simply dried grapes. As such they come in a variety of colors including light green and dark brown. They can be sun dried or mechanically dried. The most used varieties of raisins are from the Thompson seedless, Zante and Muscat grapes. Raisins are packaged in several ways. There are now **baker's raisins** which are a very moist raisin and don't have to be presoaked to add moisture to them.

Releasing Agents do exactly what they imply. They get products out of pans. The two basic types are those based on lecithin as their main ingredient and those based on an oil/flour mixture. Each is sprayed out of a can and has its own uses. They are used in place of greasing or greasing and flouring baking pans.

Rosemary belongs to the mint family and originated in the Mediterranean area where it grows wild. It now grows all over Europe and the United States. This herb, with its pungent flavor, is a favorite savory herb and can be used in sweet goods also.

Rum is liquor distilled from sugar cane juice or molasses. The majority is from the Caribbean and comes in a variety of colors from **white** or **silver rum, to golden** and **amber** rums. The darkest, most intensely flavored rum is **dark rum,** is Jamaican or Cuban. **Meyers Dark Rum** is a popular brand in the United States and the one used here.

Salt is used to bring out the flavor of ingredients. It is used less in baking than in cooking. It has long been used as a preservative. Much of today's salt is mined from deposits left by dried salt lakes around the world. There are many types of salt including table, kosher, sea, rock, and pickling and seasoned as well as colored salts. While the human body needs salt, too much can be a hindrance to good health. Table salt is used in this book.

Sugar refers to a variety of sweeteners, most commonly manufactured from sugar cane or sugar beets as used in a bakery. **Granulated sugar** (white sugar) comes in a variety of grinds. **Powdered sugar**, also known as **confectioners' sugar,** is labeled with a number of X's with the highest being the finest powder. Powdered sugar dissolves very readily and is used to make icings. **Baker's sugar** is a superfine sugar that dissolves easily when creaming or making meringue. While readily available to bakers, it is difficult to find for consumers. It can be made by putting regular granulated sugar in a processor and processing to make a finer sugar. Regular granulated sugar is coarser. **Brown sugar**, which is granulated sugar to which a varying amount of molasses has been added, has a different taste than granulated sugar. Brown sugar comes in light, medium and dark depending upon the amount of molasses added. They can be used interchangeably with little difference. However, brown sugar can dry out and become as hard as a brick. Because the molasses makes this sugar fluffier, it is necessary to pack it into measuring cups if not weighing. Microwaving very briefly can soften it again.

Decorating sugars come in sanding sugar and crystal sugar and can be found in cake decorating shops and gourmet markets. **Colored sugars** are widely available or can be made by adding a few drops of food coloring to sugar, putting a lid on the container and shaking to distribute the color.

Tequila is made by fermenting and distilling the sweet sap of the agave plant. It is made in the town of Tequila, Mexico. To be classified as tequila, it must be distilled from the blue agave in five specially delineated Mexican states. Tequila labeled "100% Blue Agave" is considered to be the best. Mexican Law requires that tequila must be made with at least 51 percent blue agave with the remainder usually being sugarcane.

Vanilla is one of the most, if not the most, used flavorings in baking. Both the extract and the whole beans, which are long, thin pods, are the byproduct of one orchid are used. The whole beans are often slit and the paste within them consisting of very small seeds are scraped out and used as the flavoring. After using the whole beans, they may be rinsed, allowed to dry and reused. The three most used types today are Bourbon-Madagascar, Mexican and Tahitian. The **Boubon-Madagascar vanilla beans** come from Africa and the Indian island of Reunion. They are the most used vanilla beans and are the thinnest of the three considered to be rich and sweet. **Mexican vanilla beans** are thicker with a smooth, rich flavor and come from around Veracruz. However, the areas where they once grew in abundance are being replaced by oil fields and orange groves. Mexican vanilla beans can contain a potentially toxic substance, coumarin, banned by the USDA and Europe as it can cause liver and kidney damage. There is no way to tell which beans contain this toxin and which don't so it is necessary to buy from reliable sources. **Tahitian vanilla beans** are the thickest and darkest of the three beans. They are intensely aromatic with a floral taste. It is often the chosen vanilla of professional chefs. Although I do not use it exclusively, Tahitian vanilla is my personal favorite lending an unusual taste to simple items, such as ice cream, pastry cream, sauces and sables. **Vanilla sugar**, often used in baking, can be made by burying several vanilla beans in a canister of sugar and letting the canister sit for a week or so. The beans can be used over and over. For a full paper on vanilla, go to my blog, www.theardentcook.com and enter vanilla in the search box.

Equipment

What you need to
make these happen

Equipment

(go to www.europeantarts.com for photographs of the equipment)

The equipment shown here is my personal equipment. Some of the equipment is new; some has been with me for many years. The important thing is not that you use what I do, but what works for you in each of the categories. Buy the best you can and the equipment will last a lifetime, as you will see in some of these pictures.

I am not a believer in buying equipment for the sake of it, especially when it comes to small wares. When I remodeled my kitchen, I put all of my small utensils in a box and whatever I didn't use in six months, I donated to a resale shop. I used exactly one item and I don't even remember what that was.

Baking sheets – Heavy sheets are important for even browning and to keep items from browning or burning before baking is completed. Professionally we used rimmed full sheet and half sheet pans that have a 1/2 to 3/4 inch rim all the way around the pan for everything including cookies. I still use half sheets in my personal kitchen to help keep the amount of equipment to a minimum. **Cookie sheets** have upturned ends but open sides.

Bowls – Several of each size of assorted bowls.

Colander – This utensil comes in plastic as well as aluminum and stainless steel and has feet to hold it above a surface. It is used primarily to let liquids drain from a product. It is particularly useful for washing and draining fruit, vegetables and pasta.

Cutting Boards – come in a variety of sizes and weights. Heavier ones will last longer and provide more stability. Placing a wet towel under the board will prevent it from moving while it is being used.

Double Boiler – This specialized piece of equipment consists of one pan seated inside of a second pan with room for water in the bottom pan. Water is added to the bottom pan so the contents of the upper pan can be warmed or cooked gently without direct heat to keep it from breaking or burning. Placing a bowl over a pan of simmering water is an alternative.

Dishers/scoopers – These are used for portion control and ease of shaping or dropping bakery items. They come in a variety of sizes with the highest size number being the smallest content size.

Food Processor –A food processor is an indispensible piece of equipment that changed how we cooked and baked when it was introduced in 1970 by Carl Sontheimer who brought it over from France. While it will not do everything, it minces, chops, mixes, purees, kneads bread dough, dices, slices, shreds and grinds a variety of foods. It is efficient and very fast, taking much of the time consuming aspects out of cooking and baking. There are various sizes of machines and motors and most of them come with several different blades, grating and slicing attachments. Because the blade turns about 30 miles an hour, it often requires recipes to be put together differently than when using a mixer. The tasks this machine can perform are amazing. But there are some caveats. It doesn't puree as good as a blender and nuts can be turned into butters or cut too finely in seconds. The pulse button can save you from disaster. The size of the motors vary as well as the capacity of the bowls. Processors usually come with several blades including an S shaped blade that chops and purees and several discs for slicing and shredding. The more powerful machines can make bread dough. A feed tube on the lid of the plastic bowl allows food to be added while the machine is running. This is a real workhorse and a great piece of equipment for the sweet kitchen.

Knives – Good knives will last a lifetime. They don't have to be the most expensive knives on the market but they should be balanced and hold a sharp edge. Essential knives include a paring knife, a chef's knife in a length you can easily use and a good bread knife with a serrated blade making it indispensable for cutting desserts.

Grater – A box grater has many uses in the kitchen but I favor a microplaner for the baking/pastry kitchen.

Heat Gun or Blowtorch – Used to heat the sides of pans to aid in the releasing of an item from its pan. This piece of equipment is particularly useful when removable rims are used. The pan is put on a can. The rim is then heated with the heat gun or blowtorch enabling the rim to be easily pushed down.

Juicer – This aluminum juicer is probably the oldest, ugliest juicer ever, but I love it. The look of this is a testament to never putting aluminum items in a dishwasher. There are many versions of juicers including electric ones. This is a simple version where the cut citrus fruit is put on top of the juicer and twisted and pressed down to extract the juice while leaving the seeds behind.

Ladles of different sizes are useful for portion control or to move liquids. They come in different sizes and professional ladles are marked in ounces.

Measuring cups – come in wet and dry measures. The wet measures have graduated sizes on them and are used for liquids, which is why there is usually a lip on the top. They come in sizes from 1 cup up to 1 gallon. I have seen them in metal, ceramic, glass and plastic. Dry measures are used for any dry ingredient. The important thing here is to overfill the cup and sweep the excess off with the back of a knife or any flat utensil.

While cups are fine for some items, weighing dry ingredients is used by professionals and is encouraged for pastry/baking success.

Measuring spoons – used to measure small amounts of ingredients. They come in a variety of sizes held together on a ring.

Microplaner – This is one of the most wonderful tools in a kitchen. Microplaners can be used to grate citrus rinds, chocolate, nutmeg, etc. They are particularly good as they remove the zest from citrus fruits without taking the bitter white pith underneath. They also keep the zest dry.

Mixer – this is a necessary piece of equipment for pastry making. It is used to combine, beat or whip ingredients. There are hand mixers and stand mixers that go from 4 1/2 quarts to huge 140-quart commercial mixers. Generally speaking, hand mixers do not have enough power for many baking and pastry applications. Stand mixers have more power and in addition to performing baking and pastry tasks, many come with attachments that enable them to perform even more tasks such as grinding meat, stuffing sausage, juicing citrus, crushing ice and making pasta. Most of the stand mixers come with a paddle, whisk and dough hook for making bread. I use a 5-quart KitchenAid mixer but have also used Cuisinart and Kenmore mixers. All of my recipes are figured for a 5-quart mixer.

Pancake Turners – are used to move tarts to their boards or platters. Two sturdy turners are placed, one on each side, to lift the tart and move it into place.

Pastry Bags – are used in conjunction with pastry tips to finish pastries. They can be plastic, cloth or disposable plastic and come in various sizes. Disposable plastic bags are used professionally to avoid cleanliness issues. If large, they can be cut down. If you use a non-disposable bag, it should be turned inside out and washed in warm soapy water and

thoroughly dry before being stored.

Pastry Brushes – come in a variety of widths and sizes. They are useful for washing down the sides of pans, brushing flour away, applying glazes and more. While expensive, it is best to use natural bristles. The plastic bristle brushes can melt on a hot pan.

Pastry Tips – are used with pastry bags. The tips used in this book include #5 and #8 open star, #48 basket weave and #1 and #5 ateco plain tip.

Quiche pans- *See tart pans with removable bottoms.*

Ruler - Any ruler, plastic or metal can be used.

Saucepans – Several sizes of pans including small to medium are used. Heavy pans will not only last a lifetime but also prevent items from burning and allow more even heat distribution.

Scales- my mantra is scales, scales, and scales. Not only for accuracy but also for speed. It is so much faster to weigh ingredients than to measure with spoons and cups. Since successful baking and pastry depend upon the accuracy of measurements, scales provide a foolproof way of measuring. No professional should ever measure with anything but a scale. However, in the spirit of compromise for home cooks, if you don't use a scale, stir the flour briefly in the bag or canister as it settles when shipping or upon sitting. Dip a dry measure into the flour and fill to overflowing; sweep off the excess.

Scissors – A sturdy pair will last longer and complete more tasks easily.

Scrapers - Scrapers are indispensible tools for baking and pastry. The **bench scraper** was originally used to scrape flour off the area used to make bread, which is referred to as a bench – hence bench scraper. In addition to scraping clean a work area, this scraper can be used to cut dough into pieces. A **bowl scraper is** used to get everything out of a mixing bowl. It is plastic and has a curved side and a flat side. The curved side is used to scrape out the sides and bottom of a bowl.

Spatulas, Metal – Large and small metal spatulas are important for frosting cakes and releasing items from pans.

Spatulas, Metal, Offset – Off set spatulas in both large, small and pointed are important for frosting cakes, particularly finishing the top, spreading any number of items out and releasing items from pans. The pointy one is useful for scalloped edge pans such as the pans used in this book.

Spatulas, Rubber – Various sizes are available. From narrow to wide from about 13 inches to 20 inches long, they serve a variety of duties in the baking/pastry kitchen. Do not use regular rubber spatulas in hot items. There are specially made high heat spatulas for use in hot pots.

Spoons of various sizes are useful from small tasting spoons to larger ones used to stir ingredients together.

Strainer – A variety of strainers in different mesh sizes are useful many tasks including straining, washing fresh fruit and sprinkling powdered sugar among other things. They often come in sets of varying sizes.

Tart pans with removable bottoms – Also referred to as quiche pans, these short tart pans with fluted rims usually have sides that are 3/4 to 1 inch tall. The bottoms come out which makes anything in them very easy to release without turning the pan upside down. These come in various sizes from 3 1/2 inches, which is the smallest pan I have used to 12" round. I have also seen them in square and rectangular pans.

Thermometers – There are a variety of thermometers for different uses. Freezer and refrigerator thermometers are important to keep track of the temperatures for safety.

Freezers should be kept at 0 degrees or below. Refrigerators should be kept between 33 and 40 degrees. A candy thermometer registers high temperatures used in candy and sugar work.

An instant read thermometer records temperatures very quickly. The temperature ranges can vary.

Toothpicks and Skewers – These are used to finish desserts.

Vegetable Peeler – There are basically two styles of peelers available, the straight or the Y shaped. My preference is the straight, swivel bladed version that has a rounded end for digging out the eyes of potatoes or other produce. The important thing here is to find one that is comfortable in your hand.

Whisks – can be used for various tasks in the kitchen, including mixing and whipping ingredients. They come in very fine wire to heavy wire depending upon the use. They also come in various heights to accommodate different size containers.

Weights and Measurement Chart

My best case
for a scale!

Weights And Measurement Chart

These are the weights of the major items in this book.

Almond Paste .... **1 cup = 225 grams or 8 ounces**

Baking Powder .... **1 teaspoon =5 grams or .20 ounce**

Butter

1 pound= 2 cups .... **454 grams**

4 sticks .... **454 grams or 16 ounces**

1 stick .... **114 grams or 4 ounces**

1 Tablespoon .... **15 grams or 1/2 ounce**

Caramel .... **1 cup = 300 grams or 10 ounces**

Cinnamon .... **1 teaspoon=3 grams or .095 ounce**

Cocoa

Cocoa, unsifted .... 1 cup = 85 grams or 3 ounces

Cocoa, sifted .... 1 cup = 70 grams or 2 1/3 ounce

Coconut, sweetened .... 1 cup = 85 grams or 3 ounce

Corn Syrup

1 cup ....255 grams or 8 ounces

1 tablespoon .... 17 grams or .040 ounce

Cream of Coconut ....1 cup = 280 grams or 10 ounces

Cup to Gram Conversion

1 ounce = 28.34 grams (often rounded to 30 grams)

1 pound = 454 grams or 16 ounces

1 gram =.035 ounce

1 teaspoon = 5 milliliters

1 tablespoons = 15 milliliters

1 fluid ounce = 29.57 milliliters or 2 tablespoons

1 fluid cup = 236.56 milliliters or 16 tablespoons

Eggs (as used in this book)

Whole ....58 grams or 2 ounces

Egg yolk .... 17 grams or .67 ounce

Egg white .... 32 grams or 1.8 ounces

Flour

Cake Flour, unsifted.. 1 cup = 125 grams or 4 1/3 ounces

Cake Flour, sifted..1 cup = 100 grams or 3 1/2 ounces

All Purpose Flour, unsifted..1 cup = 140 grams or 5 ounces

All Purpose Flour, sifted.. 1 cup = 114 grams or 4 ounces

Gelatin.. 1 teaspoon= 3 grams or .033 ounce

Graham Cracker Crumbs.. 1 cup =140 grams or 5 ounces

Honey.. 1 cup = 340 grams or 12 ounces

Peanut Butter.. 1 cup =256 grams or 9 ounces

Raisins

Baking Raisins (moist)..1 cup = 170 grams or 6 ounces

Regular Raisin..1 cup = 135 grams or 4 3/4 ounces

Raspberry Jam, seedless..1 cup = 260 grams or 9 ounces

Salt..5 grams or .20 ounces

Sour Cream..1 cup = 225 grams or 8 ounces

Sugar

Brown Sugar, ...1 cup = 200 grams or 7 ounces

Granulated sugar...1 cup = 200 grams or 7 ounces

Powdered sugar, unsifted .... 1 cup = 114 grams or 4 ounces

Powdered sugar, sifted.............................. .... 1 cup = 90 grams or 3 ounces

Water.. .... 1 cup 225 grams or 8 ounces

Top, Margarita Tart, page 26
Bottom, S'Mores Tart, page 76

Crusts

Getting to the bottom of tarts

Press In Crusts

General Notes on Press-in Crusts

Plain Press-In Shell

Chocolate Press-In Shell

Basic Graham Cracker Crust

Chocolate Graham Cracker Crumb Crust

General Notes On Press-In Crusts

These crusts are the main ones used in this book. The first of these crusts is of the "cookie crust" variety that are pressed into the shell, baked partially or fully and then filled. If partially baked, they are filled and baked with the filling. These crusts shrink so little there is no need to weight them down. This type of crust is ideal for these particular tarts because most of them require refrigeration and the crusts do not become soggy. They retain their crispness for days even under refrigeration or after freezing and thawing. These come in a plain and chocolate version.

The second crust is of the graham cracker variety. The chocolate variation was developed to avoid buying expensive chocolate cookies. It uses graham cracker crumbs, cocoa and powdered sugar as its base. We made this in 35 pound batches and stored it in plastic containers until we needed it. Then we simply weighed what we needed for as many crusts as we wanted, added melted butter and we were ready to go. These crusts were rarely baked.

The four most used crusts are included here. The general rule for the crumb crust is 2/3 of the crumbs are used for the sides and 1/3 for the bottom of the tart. At the bakery we pressed them in and froze them in freezer proof bags, to be used as needed. I do not recommend baking the plain and chocolate press-in crusts and then freezing them as they have a tendency to crack if not filled. Besides they are fresher if they are just baked and then filled. Some recipes call for partially baking the crust if they are to be filled and baked again. If the tart will not be baked again, then the crust should be completely baked.

11" Plain Press-In Pastry

(go to www.europeantarts.com, Chocolate Press- in Pastry, for how to photographs)

1 1/4 cups sifted all-purpose flour (170 grams or 6 ounces)
1/2 cup sifted cake flour (50 grams or 1 3/4 ounces)
1/2 teaspoon baking powder
1 stick unsalted butter, cold and cut into small pieces (114 grams or 4 ounces)
1/4 cup sugar (50 grams or 1 3/4 ounces)
1 egg
1 egg yolk
Preheat oven to 350 degrees if baking immediately.

Mixer Method: Combine the flours, baking powder and butter in mixer bowl. Beat with the paddle attachment until the butter is cut in very finely. Add the sugar; mix briefly. Add the egg and yolk; mix on medium speed until it comes together in a ball.

Food Processor Method: Place the flours and baking powder in the food processor. Process to mix briefly. Place the butter in a circle over the flours. Process until finely cut in. Add the sugar; process briefly. Add the egg and yolk and process until a ball forms.

Spray only the center bottom of the pan only with a releasing spray. Divide the dough in half (175 grams or 6 ounces). Divide one piece in half again (85 grams or 3 ounces). Roll one quarter of the dough (85 grams or 3 ounces) evenly into a rope. Lay against one half edge of the pan. Repeat with the other quarter, overlapping the pieces slightly. Press into the side of the shell, sealing the two pieces together. Flatten the remaining half of the dough into a circle. Place it in the bottom of the pan. With the heel of your hand, press the dough outward toward the edge. Continue to work the dough outward with your fingers and lastly, seal the seam. Be sure to seal the seam well where the edge and the bottom meet so it does not crack when baked. Prick the tart bottom with a fork. Place on a baking sheet and bake for 12 to 15 minutes if partially baking or 18 to 22 minutes until a rich golden brown if fully baking. Cool; fill and finish as directed.

Weight of full crust before baking is 350 grams or 12 1/4 ounces.

To make individual shells

3 1/2" individual shells are 40 grams (1 1/2 ounces) each. Use 25 grams (1 scant ounce) for the sides and 15 grams (1/2 ounce) for the bottom of each shell.
4 3/4" individual shells are 60 grams (2 ounces) each. Use 35 (1 heavy ounce) for the sides and 25 grams (1 scant ounce) for the bottom.
Bake at 350 degrees 12 to 15 minutes for partially baked, 18 to 20 minutes for fully baked.

9" Plain-Press In Pastry

(go to www.europeantarts.com , Chocolate Press-In Pastry, for how to photographs)

3/4 cup all-purpose flour (114 grams or 4 ounces)
1/3 cup cake flour (35 grams or 1 1/4 ounces)
6 tablespoons unsalted butter, cold and cut into small pieces (58 grams or 2 ounces)
3 tablespoons sugar (25 grams or 1 scant ounce)
1/3 teaspoon baking powder
1 egg

See directions above.

Chocolate Press-In Pastry

(go to www.euroopeantarts.com for how to photographs for the plain crust)

For one 11"x1" quiche pan.

1 1/4 cups all purpose flour (140 grams or 5 ounces)
1/2 cup cake flour (50 grams or 1 3/4 scant ounce)
¼ cup cocoa (20 grams or 3/4 ounce)
1/2 teaspoon baking powder
1 stick butter, cold and cut into pieces (114 grams or 4 ounces)
1/2 cup sugar (100 grams or 3 1/2 ounces)
1 egg
1 egg yolk
Preheat oven to 350 degrees if baking immediately.

Mixer Method: Combine flours, cocoa and baking powder in mixing bowl. Mix briefly to combine. Add the butter and cut in with the paddle attachment until very fine. Add the sugar; mix to combine. Add the egg and yolk; mix until a ball forms.

Processor Method: Place flours, cocoa and baking powder in food processor. Place butter in a circle over flours. Process until finely cut in. Add sugar and process briefly to mix. Add egg and yolk and process until a ball forms.

Spray the center of the bottom of the pan. Divide the dough in half (200 grams or 7 ounces). Divide one half into half again (2 - 100 grams or 3 1/2 ounce pieces). Roll one quarter of the dough (100 grams or 3 1/2 ounces) into a rope that will fit half way around the edge of the pan. Press the dough evenly along the side. Repeat with the remaining quarter and press against the other side of the pan, overlapping the edges and pressing firmly together. Use the remaining dough and press in the bottom sealing the edges together very well. Prick the tart bottom. Bake approximately 10 minutes for partially baked and about 15 minutes for a fully baked shell.

Yield: 400 grams

9" Chocolate Graham Cracker Crumb Crust

(go to www.europeantarts.com for how to photographs)

1 1/3 cups graham cracker crumbs (buy them in crumbs or run the crackers through food processor) (170 grams or 6 ounces)
¼ cup cocoa (25 grams or 1 scant ounce)
½ cup unsifted powdered sugar (55 grams or 2 ounces)
10 tablespoons unsalted butter, melted (150 grams or 5 1/3 ounces)

Sift the cocoa and powdered sugar together in a bowl. Add the crumbs, mixing well. Add the butter and toss with a fork until the crumbs are completely coated. Spray the bottom of the quiche pan and press 2/3 of the crumbs (200 grams or 7 ounces) evenly over the bottom of the pan. Distribute them evenly against the sides. Press firmly against sides. Add the remainder (160 grams or 5 2/3 ounces) on the bottom and press firmly.

Notes: We used dutched cocoa at the shop but non-dutched is also fine. If you are making a lot of the mixture, place the dry ingredients in the bowl of a mixer and blend with the whisk attachment to remove any lumps in the powdered sugar or cocoa. If you are crushing the graham crackers in a food processor, simply add the powdered sugar and cocoa processing to mix. In either case, add the butter by hand.

One recipe will make:

6 – 3 1/2" individual tart shells – 25 grams (1 scant ounce) for the sides and 15 grams (1/2 ounce) for the bottom or

4 – 4 3/4" individual tart shells – 50 grams (1 2/3 ounces) for the sides and 25 grams (1 scant ounce for the bottoms.

9" Basic Graham Cracker Crumb Crust

(go to www.europeantarts.com, 9" Chocolate Graham Cracker Crumb Crust for how photographs)

Omit the cocoa, reduce the butter to 8 tablespoons (114 grams or 4 ounces) and add 1/2 teaspoon vanilla. Mix and press in as above.

Left, Chocolate Raspberry Truffle Tart, page 60
Top, Orange Blossom Tart, page 28
Bottom Right, Lemon Raspberry Tart, page 24

Curd Tarts

No Whey!

Curd Tarts

General Notes On Curds

Curds in general are thick, creamy mixtures of fruit juices or whole fruits with sugar and butter thickened with egg yolks. However they can be tricky to make. By understanding the nature of curds and adding an additional ingredient, runny curds are a thing of the past. As I hired more employees, it was sometimes difficult for everyone to know when the curd had reached its maximum ability to thicken. Safeguards, in the way of a uniform recipe had to be found. Over cooking it or raising the temperature of the curd too quickly risks the chance of breaking it – at which point it will not thicken. That is why the butter is always put in cold – to slow the heat. By placing the ingredients for the curd over a double boiler it lessens the chance of raising the temperature of the curd too quickly. Additionally the use of an instant read thermometer will enable you to maximize the thickening at the perfect point before it gets too hot.

Egg yolks have traditionally been the only thickener used for curds. In my first book, The New Pastry Cook, 1986 by William Morrow Co., I gave a recipe for Lemon Curd that added a bit of gelatin that will guarantee a firm curd every time. The gelatin also makes it possible to pipe the curd without it breaking down. Without the gelatin, the curd will hold its points at first when piped but as it is worked the curd loosens and no longer pipes well.

The secret of good, firm curd is to move it around as little as possible after it has chilled. However, stirring too much at any point after it has set can cause it to break down. After cooking, cover the surface of the curd directly with plastic wrap to prevent a crust from forming on top. We used curds for tart and cake fillings as well as piped petit fours. As long as you don't overwork it, it will be fine. The curd holds in the refrigerator for a week to 10 days and the finished products using curds freeze well.

To make it easier to juice lemons, limes, or oranges, microwave the lemons for 20 seconds, the limes for 15 seconds and the oranges for 30 seconds before squeezing. Sometimes grated lemon zest is used to enhance the lemony taste of lemon curd. I prefer the creamy smoothness of the curd without the little bumps caused by the zest - especially don't use zest if you are going to pipe the curd as the zest gets hung up in the piping tip.

You will notice all of the curd tarts are topped in some way to protect the curd.

If the tarts are stored several days in the refrigerator, as they often are when used in restaurants, the curd will often dry out and crack. Covering the curd prevents this.

All of the curd tarts freeze beautifully with the exception of the fresh fruit tarts. In this case, freeze the filled tarts without the fruit. Thaw in the refrigerator and several hours prior to serving, top with the fruit. Store in the refrigerator.

Cranberry Curd

(go to www.europeantarts.com for how to photographs)

This had become an absolute favorite for the holidays. Besides its' vibrant color, the taste and texture are outstanding. We used it in tarts, cakes and petit fours. Room permitting, we would freeze cases of cranberries at the end of the season in order to get a head start the following season and test new recipes during the year. Pick over the cranberries for the odd ones that need to be discarded. To prevent them from rolling all over your kitchen (like they did in ours before we figured this out), place them in a jelly roll pan or rimmed baking sheet where they will be in one layer. You can see all of them and shaking the pan will turn them over to make sure no bad ones are hiding. It saves a lot of time chasing them around the floor. They have a way of going directly under the most difficult area to reach. Cranberries have so much natural pectin; this sets up very firmly without the addition of gelatin.

12 ounce bag fresh or frozen cranberries picked over
1 cup sugar (7 ounces or 200 grams)
2 tablespoons water
5 egg yolks (3 ounces or 85 grams)
1 tablespoon lemon juice
1 stick unsalted butter, cold and cut into pieces (4 ounces or 114 grams)

Cook the cranberries with sugar and water over low heat until the cranberries are very soft and some of them have popped. Stir frequently as this will be very thick and can scorch.

Immediately, puree them in a food processor (by batches if necessary). Puree for several minutes to get the skins as fine as possible. There will be tiny specs of red which is as it should be. If you prefer to remove the skins, strain the puree before proceeding. Add the yolks and lemon juice to the processor and process briefly. Place the cranberry mixture in the top of a double boiler and add the butter. Bring the water underneath to a boil. Stir the curd constantly until an instant read thermometer reads 170 degrees.

Use as directed at once or store in refrigerator with the top covered directly with plastic wrap.

Yield: 2 1/4 cups

Chocolate Cranberry Curd Tart

(go to www.europeantarts.com for how to photographs)

Perfect for the holidays, this is an unusual combination of color and textures. This curd will never be as smooth as a lemon or lime curd because the skins of the cranberries do not puree perfectly smooth. However, it is this very thing that adds texture to the taste. In contrast, the chocolate glaze is as smooth as silk. This is a much firmer curd than any of the others and has no trouble sitting at room temperature for several hours. Many of our clients waited for November and December when we featured this sleek looking dessert.

11" Chocolate Press-in Shell
1 batch Cranberry Curd, freshly made

Pour the cranberry curd into the shell and cover directly with plastic wrap. Place in the refrigerator overnight to firm.

Chocolate Cream Glaze

3/4 cup 40% cream
6 ounces semisweet chocolate, cut into small pieces (170 grams)

Bring the cream to a simmer. Remove from the heat and submerge the chocolate under the cream. Allow to sit for 4 or 5 minutes then whisk gently to smooth chocolate.

Remove the wrap from the top of the tart and pour the glaze over the curd just to the edge of the curd. Chill 20 to 25 minutes to set the glaze. Release and cut into 10 to 12 servings. The tart may be refrigerated overnight or frozen for longer storage.

Lemon Curd

(go to www.europeantarts.com for how to photographs)

This is a very tart sweet lemon curd with plenty of lemon taste.

1 teaspoon water
1/2 teaspoon gelatin
2 whole eggs
3 egg yolks
1/2 cup sugar (100 grams or 3 1/2 ounces)
1/2 cup lemon juice, freshly squeezed - do not use the bottle version
1 stick cold butter, cut in pieces (114 grams or 4 ounces)

Dissolve the gelatin in the water. Set aside.

Place the eggs and yolks in the top of a double boiler. Whisk to combine. Whisk in the sugar and lemon juice. Add the butter pieces. Place over hot water and, stirring constantly, bring to 172 degrees on a candy thermometer. Tear the dissolved gelatin into little pieces and whisk into the curd.

Use at once or pour into a storage container, cover the surface with plastic wrap; poke a few holes in it and refrigerate to cool.

Yield: 1 2/3 cups or 454 grams or 16 ounces.

Lime Curd: Substitute lime juice (freshly squeezed) for the lemon juice. You will need 3 to 4 medium size limes. The lime curd will not be green. I prefer not to use coloring agents unless absolutely necessary. Add a drop or two of food coloring if you prefer it green.

Fresh Blueberry Lemon Tart, page 23

Fresh Blueberry Lemon Tart

There is nothing like fresh fruit in season. Team it up with a zesty lemon curd and you have the makings of an outstanding dessert. At the shop we had a special emulsified powdered sugar that does not melt in the refrigerator. We use it to dust many of our tarts. However, if you use regular powdered sugar dust it just before serving as it melts in the refrigerator or freezer upon thawing.

11" Plain Press-In Shell
1 batch of Lemon Curd, freshly made
1 pint of fresh blueberries
Powdered sugar

Pour the lemon curd into the shell just under the top. There will be a bit leftover. Cover the surface with plastic wrap and chill in the refrigerator overnight. Release from the pan.

Shortly before serving, remove the wrap from the tart and starting at the outside edge arrange the blueberries in concentric circles. If there are not enough to completely cover the tart, it is just as attractive with the lemon curd showing in the middle. Refrigerate.

Just before serving, dust with powdered sugar.

To serve: Cut into 10 to 12 servings.

To make ahead: The tart may be made and frozen after it is filled with lemon curd. Thaw in the refrigerator the day before. Finish as above.

Lemon Raspberry Tart

(go to www.europeantarts.com for how to photographs)

Without a doubt this was one of the three top-selling products we made. During the entertaining months of the year we were hard pressed to keep up with demand. It is important to use a good quality white chocolate that is made with cocoa butter. Do not use white chocolate coating, which uses palm or coconut oil as it doesn't melt and blend the same not to mention the taste.

11" Plain-Press in crust, fully baked
1/2 cup good quality, seedless red raspberry jam or preserves (130 grams or 4 1/2 ounces)
1 batch Lemon Curd, freshly made
Fortified Raspberry Jam for piping, below
White Chocolate Glaze, below

Spread the bottom of the shell with the raspberry jam. Make the lemon curd and pour it not quite to the top of the shell. Leave a bit of room for the glaze. There will be some curd left. Cover the surface of the curd directly with plastic wrap. Refrigerate several hours until firm or overnight. Release from the pan.

Fortified Raspberry Jam for Chevron

2 teaspoons water
1/2 teaspoon gelatin
1/2 cup seedless red raspberry jam or preserves

Sprinkle the gelatin over the cold water. Place the jam in a small saucepan and bring it to a simmer. Microwave the gelatin to liquefy it and stir it into the jam. Cover with film and refrigerate for several hours or until set up.

White Chocolate Glaze

7 ounces white chocolate, cut into small pieces (200 grams)
1/3 cup 40% cream

Place the chocolate and cream in the top of a double boiler; set aside. In the bottom of a double boiler, bring several inches of water to a rapid boil. Remove from the heat and immediately place the top of the double boiler on the bottom pan. Do not cover. Allow the chocolate to melt stirring often and whisking to smooth the chocolate. Remove the plastic wrap from the tart and pour the glaze over the middle of the filling. With a small offset spatula move the glaze lightly from the middle just to the edge of the filling sealing in the lemon curd.

Place the fortified raspberry filling in a piping bag fitted with a #5 small ateco tip. Immediately pipe straight lines left to right across the tart, starting about 1 inch from the top. Continue down the tart leaving about 1 1/2 inches between the lines. You should have 9 lines. With a toothpick or bamboo skewer, starting close to the left side lightly draw a straight line from the top to the bottom through the raspberry lines. At the bottom, move over about 1 inch and draw the line straight up from the bottom to the top. Repeat across the tart going down and up to form the chevron design. Store in the refrigerator or freeze.

Release and cut into 10 to 12 servings.

Lemon Curd Tart: Omit the raspberry jam on the bottom of the shell for the Lemon Raspberry Tart. White chocolate glaze drizzled with dark chocolate or whipped cream should finish the top to prevent the curd from drying out.

Margarita Tart

(go to www.europeantarts.com for how to photographs)

Summers in St. Louis are often hot and humid and the taste of lime helps cut the heat. This perky little tart is the perfect ending to a grilled or barbecued dinner especially one with a southwestern theme. The finish resembles little cacti. Can you tell I love how this looks and tastes?

11" Plain Press-in Shell, completely baked
1 batch Lime Curd, freshly made

Pour lime curd into tart shell just to the top. There will be a bit left over; store separately. Cover surface of tart directly with plastic wrap and chill several hours to set or overnight in the refrigerator. Release from the pan.

Topping

1 cup 40% cream
6 tablespoons powdered sugar (45 grams or 1 1/2 ounces)
2 tablespoons clear tequila

Combine all the ingredients and beat until stiff peaks form.

Release the tart. Fit a pastry bag with a number 6B tip. Pipe small stars of whipped cream to cover the tart. Fit another pastry bag with a #1 writing tip and fill the bag with lime curd. Dot the top of each star with curd. Refrigerate or freeze.

To Serve: Cut into 10 to 12 pieces.

Orange Curd

While the use of gelatin in the lemon and lime curd is not strictly necessary, the use of it here is definitely a necessity. This is a most interesting curd as when it is completely cooked, it is still very, very liquid. Do not panic at this point (like I did). It will set up perfectly upon chilling. The use of lemon juice in addition to the orange juice and rind gives the requisite tartness to this curd. The rind is necessary here to reinforce the juice, which is not as assertive as lemon or lime. Microwave the lemon for 15 to 20 seconds and the orange for 30 seconds to make the juicing much easier as the fruit readily gives up its juice when the fruit is warm.

2 tablespoons lemon juice
1 teaspoon gelatin
6 egg yolks (3 1/2 ounces or 100 grams)
1/2 cup sugar (3 1/2 ounces or 100 grams
1 1/2 tablespoons orange rind
2/3 cup orange juice
6 tablespoons butter (3 ounces or 85 grams)

Dissolve the gelatin in the lemon juice. Set aside.
Beat the egg yolks in the top of a double boiler to mix; whisk in the sugar.

Add the orange rind and juice; mix well. Add the butter; place over hot water in a double boiler and cook, stirring constantly, until the mixture reaches 172 degrees on a candy thermometer. Tear the dissolved gelatin into small pieces and whisk into the curd. Use immediately as directed or cover directly with film; poke a few holes in it and allow to cool, then refrigerate. This will last 10 days in a refrigerator and freezes well.

Yield: 1 2/3 cup

Orange Blossom Tart

(go to www.europeantarts.com for how to photographs)

This tart employs both orange curd and pastry cream for a stunning looking, outrageously tasty dessert. This dessert was designed by one of my employees, Kenda Morado.

11" Plain Press-In Shell, fully baked
1 batch of Orange Curd, freshly made

Fill the shell with the orange curd to just below the top. There will be some curd left. Cover directly with film and refrigerate overnight to firm.

Topping

1 batch pastry cream, chilled *(see the Pastry Cream chapter)*
1/2 cup 40% cream
1/3 cup powdered sugar (40 grams or a scant 1 1/2 ounces)
1/2 teaspoon vanilla

Whisk the pastry cream until smooth. Do not over whisk. Set aside. Place remaining ingredients in a mixing bowl fitted with a whisk attachment. Beat until the cream is very stiff. Fold the pastry cream and whipped cream together. Fit a pastry bag with a #8 star tip.

Release the tart and remove the film from the tart. Pipe two rows of large rosettes to cover the top of the orange curd. If it does not completely cover the tart, that's fine. Refrigerate or freeze.

Cut into 10 to 12 servings.

Left, Apricot Crumble Tart, page 39
Right, Café au Lait Truffle Tart, page 48

Pastry Cream

The go-to filling
for pastries

Pastry Cream Tarts

General Notes On Pastry Cream

Of French derivation, pastry cream or crème patisserie is a custard-like cousin of the sauce crème anglaise. There are myriad variations that can flavor the basic version including chocolate - white or dark, coffee, liqueurs, citrus zest or coconut. Base ingredients can vary including whole eggs or egg yolks only, cream, half and half or milk, cornstarch or flour. The noted Pastry Chef/Instructor Bo Friberg describes it best in his book, The Professional Pastry Chef: "Making pastry cream is one of the basic techniques that anyone involved with cooking (pastry shop or otherwise) should master, because pastry cream has so many applications. In an emergency, it can be thinned and used as a sauce; it is a base for soufflé; it is a filling and flavoring for cakes; and it can be used as a topping for Danish or other pastries. In the pastry kitchen, there should always be a supply of pastry cream in the refrigerator."

Cornstarch is often used as the thickener as flour is thought to make the cream heavy or "rubbery". The problem with cornstarch is that it does not freeze well as, upon thawing, it becomes watery and breaks down. This can be avoided by using a combination of flour and gelatin, which keeps it from becoming rubbery or starchy tasting. It also allows the pastry cream to be frozen in predetermined amounts and used as needed. While Chef Friberg keeps his pastry cream in the refrigerator, we kept ours in the freezer, as we didn't use it everyday. Egg yolks only are used as an additional thickening agent. Always thaw the pastry cream in the refrigerator before using. It will need to be whisked gently by hand or machine to smooth it out. Be careful not to overbeat and break it down.

It is important to use a stainless steel or non-aluminum pot because if the pastry cream is made in an aluminum pot it will become an unappetizing gray color. Because we made this in large amounts, cooking it over direct heat was not recommended as no matter how diligently it was stirred, the bottom scorches at best, burns at worst. If this occurs do not try to keep it, as the burned flavor will permeate the entire batch. To avoid this we place the mixture over a double boiler until it reaches 190 degrees then move it to direct heat to bring it to a boil and complete the thickening. This step is not necessary if making a single recipe, as the mixture will cook quite quickly unless you are new to pastry and want to insure it comes out. Just remember to stay with it and stir constantly as cream or milk scorch easily.

Because the egg yolks are mixed only with sugar before the hot milk is introduced it is important to temper the egg yolks so you don't end up with scrambled eggs. To temper the yolks, add the hot milk very slowly in the beginning while whisking constantly. This will allow the yolks to accept the heat slowly and as the milk is introduced, it can be added faster after the first third is in.

This is a very firm pastry cream to allow whipped cream to be folded in and still hold up.

We sold 3 1/2 inch individual and 11 inch full sized tarts filled with the pastry cream, frozen and unfinished. These are called "blanks". The client could then finish them as desired and serve the freshest fruit tarts to their customers as fruit tarts have a very short life before the fruit starts looking distressed.

Pastry Cream

(go to www.europeantarts.com for how to photographs)

1 1/2 teaspoons gelatin
2 teaspoons cold water
1 1/3 cup milk, very hot
4 egg yolks
1/2 cup sugar (100 grams or 3 1/2 ounces)
1/4 cup flour (35 grams or 1 ounce)
1 teaspoon vanilla extract or 1 vanilla bean split
Soften the gelatin in the water and set aside.

If using the vanilla bean, scrape out the seeds and add to the milk along with the pod; heat the milk until hot but not boiling.

Whisk the egg yolks and sugar together in a non-reactive saucepan. Whisk in the flour. Remove the pod from the milk. Add the milk slowly, whisking well and scraping the corners of pan with a rubber spatula to make sure all of the egg yolk mixture is incorporated. Place over medium heat and, stirring constantly, bring to a boil. Boil for 1 minute, stirring constantly. Remove from the heat and add the vanilla (if using extract). Tear the dissolved gelatin into small pieces and stir it into the hot liquid (there is no need to liquefy it, the heat of the mixture will do this for you). Pour into a storage container, cover the surface with plastic wrap, poke a few holes in it and refrigerate overnight to chill or freeze.

Yield: 2 cups (490 grams or 17 ounces)

Note: If making this in a large batch you will need to portion it out to freeze. We lined 6" cake pans with film letting the film overhang the pan. We poured 2 cups or 490 grams (19 ounces) into the pan; twisted the film to seal it and placed in the freezer. When frozen, remove from the pans and place in a freezer proof bag. Thaw in the refrigerator as needed and use as desired.

Fresh Fruit Tart

It can be difficult to find what I call a "real" fruit tart. Often the filling comes out of a bucket and the glaze is sprayed out of a hose. The glaze is meant to keep the fruit from deteriorating. Since I never used glaze, we either left the fruit with nothing adorning it or sprinkled it lightly with powdered sugar. While not readily available to consumers, bakeries can use a special emulsified powdered sugar, which will not become watery when refrigerated or upon defrosting.

This tart is even better than the original because we lighten the pastry cream, which can be heavy, with a bit of whipped cream. This is actually a year round desert since any fresh, ripe, fruit is used. The only non-fresh fruit used are mandarin oranges because they add such color and are good to form borders. Use as many different kinds of fruit on one tart as you wish. There are no rules here. This is definitely a place where the more the merrier works. One last point; finish this the day it will be served. It's really a snap because the shell can be baked, filled ahead with the pastry cream and then frozen. Thaw it the night before in the refrigerator and top with the fruit shortly before serving.

The shell is fortified against becoming soggy with a layer of either chocolate or jam spread on the bottom before adding the pastry cream.

11" Plain-Press In Shell
2 ounces semisweet chocolate (60 grams)
1/2 cup good quality raspberry jam (130 grams or 4 1/2 ounces)
1 batch pastry cream, chilled
1/2 cup 40% cream
Fresh fruit of your choice.

Spread the bottom of the shell with either the chocolate or jam to help keep the shell crisp. Set aside.

Whip the cream very stiff. Whisk the pastry cream in a large bowl until smooth. Fold in the whipped cream. Spread in the shell. Release from the shell. (At this point the filling can be covered directly with plastic wrap and frozen. Thaw in the refrigerator.) Arrange the fruit as desired over the cream. Some of the pastry cream showing in the center is fine - don't worry if you run out of fruit. Cover lightly with plastic wrap and refrigerate until shortly before serving.

To serve: Sprinkle with powdered sugar and cut into 10 to 12 pieces.

Apricot Crumble Tart

(go to www.europeantarts.com for how to photographs)

The filling for this tart is reminiscent of the Hungarian filling, lekvar. It is easily made and has an intense flavor. The important point here is not to cover the pan when reconstituting the dried apricots. Most dried apricots are treated with sulfur to retain their bright color. By reconstituting the fruit in an uncovered, non-reactive pan, it allows the sulfur to escape making a much cleaner apricot taste.

Pastry Cream, chilled *(see Pastry Cream chapter)*

11" Plain Press-In shell, fully baked
Apricot Filling, below
Almond Paste Crumbs, below
1/2 cup whipping cream
1/3 cup powdered sugar (40 grams or 1 1/4 ounces)
1 teaspoon vanilla

Apricot Filling

1/2 pound dried apricots (225 grams)
2/3 cups water
3 tablespoons butter (45 grams or 1 3/4 ounces)
1/3 cup powdered sugar (40 grams or 1 1/4 ounces)
1 teaspoon vanilla

Place the apricots and water in a small non-reactive saucepan. Simmer, uncovered, stirring frequently until the water is almost gone and the apricots are soft. Place the apricots and remaining ingredients in a processor bowl and process until smooth. Set aside to cool. This can be made a week ahead and kept in the refrigerator.

Almond Paste Crumbs

1/3 cup flour (45 grams, or 1 1/2 ounces)
1/3 cup packed brown sugar (65 grams or 2 ounces)
1/2 teaspoon salt
3 tablespoons cold unsalted butter, cut into small pieces (45 grams or 1 1/2 ounces)
2 ounces almond paste (60 grams)

Preheat oven to 350 degrees.
Place all the ingredients in the food processor. Process until crumbly. Do not over process, as you want fairly large crumbs. Line a baking sheet with parchment and spread the crumbs out. Bake about 7 to 10 minutes or until golden.

Assembly

Spread the cooled apricot filling over the bottom of the baked crust.

Whip the cream with the powdered sugar and vanilla until stiff. Whisk the pastry cream to smooth and fold in the whipped cream. Spread this over the apricot filling. Top with the Almond Paste Crumbs. Chill until needed. Release and cut into 10 to 12 pieces.

Left, Chocolate Chip Truffle Tart, page 52
Right, Tropical Truffle Tart, page 61

Truffle Tarts

Where Chocoholics
go for a fix!

Truffle Tarts

General Notes On Truffle Tarts

Truffle Tarts are the easiest and most versatile of all the tarts in this book. With the exception of two crusts, there is no baking and minimal heating of ingredients - yet the end result is intense in taste and sophisticated in looks. These are ideal for those with little baking experience but a passion for desserts and equally good for restaurants and professionals tired of bread pudding, crème brulee or ice cream. A simple press-in crust is filled with a liquid chocolate mixture that sets upon refrigeration. After that, the sky's the limit with endless variations possible. These are so rich they are generally cut into 10 to 12 pieces and benefit from being removed from the refrigerator about 1 to 2 hours before serving.

The key to these tarts is not to overheat the cream or the chocolate filling will be dull. Heat the cream mixture just until steaming and the butter (if called for) melts. Immediately remove the pan from the heat and submerge the chocolate under the cream. Let it sit for 4 to 5 minutes. Stir to incorporate the chocolate, switching to a whisk to smooth it out. Do not whisk so vigorously that air bubbles are incorporated.

The choice of chocolate will affect the outcome of the filling. A good chocolate, bittersweet or semisweet, depending upon your taste, anywhere from 58% to 68% cocoa butter is ideal. We never used chocolate chips unless they were for cookies. Most chocolate companies now offer chocolate wafers or buttons. These are far more convenient than bars as you don't have to cut them up. They can go straight into the cream to melt. For many years the chocolate only came in bars, which had to be cut into small pieces to use. If you use bars, cut into small pieces and store in a covered container for use as needed. We often cut 100 pounds at a time in those days. Chocolate has come a long way in convenience since then.

This is the base recipe for a 9" truffle tart. Although the amounts of the ingredients may change for some recipes the directions remain the same. All of the truffle tarts freeze well unless otherwise noted.

Base Recipe for a 9" Chocolate Truffle Tart

1 cup 40% cream
4 tablespoons unsalted butter (58 grams or 2 ounces)
1/4 cup sugar (50 grams or 1 3/4 ounce)
10 ounces semisweet chocolate (285 grams)
1 teaspoon vanilla

Heat the cream, butter and sugar until steaming and butter is melted. Whisk gently to make sure butter is melted and sugar is dissolved. Remove from the heat and add the chocolate and vanilla submerging the chocolate under the cream. Let sit for 4 to 5 minutes. Gently whisk to smooth out the chocolate. Using a rubber spatula, go around the bottom edges of the pan to make sure all of the chocolate is melted. Use as directed.

Café Au Lait Truffle Tart

9" Chocolate Graham Cracker Crumb Crust
1 1/4 cup 40% cream
1 tablespoon instant coffee
15 ounces milk chocolate (424 grams)
1 ounce semisweet chocolate (30 grams)

Heat the cream and coffee until steaming. Do not boil. Submerge the milk chocolate below the cream. Let sit 4 to 5 minutes. Stir to incorporate chocolate, whisking towards the end to remove any lumps. Pour into the crust. Refrigerate to set; release from the pan.

Microwave the semisweet chocolate in short bursts at 50% power to melt it. Drizzle over the tart.

Cut into 10 to 12 servings.

Caramel

(go to www.europeantarts.com for how to photographs)

We used a lot of caramel at the shop and never found a smooth, buttery caramel that tasted as good and was the correct consistency without making our own. So we did! Sometimes there was so much caramel going, you would think we were a candy shop instead of a bakery. If you are not using the caramel immediately, it will keep well at room temperature when it is cool. Refrigerate it if the weather is warm or the butter will separate. To warm it for spreading, microwave briefly. Do not overheat or over stir, as the butter will separate and rise to the top. If this happens, pour off the melted butter. For any recipe calling for caramel, you can do as we did and make this several days in advance. Warm to use.

1/2 cup cold water
3/4 cup sugar (150 grams or 5 1/3 ounces)
1 tablespoon corn syrup
3 1/2 tablespoons unsalted butter
1/2 cup 40% cream, hot
1/2 teaspoon vanilla

Place the water, sugar and the corn syrup in a 2-quart saucepan. Stir over heat until the sugar is dissolved completely. Bring to a boil; wash sides of pan down with a natural bristle pastry brush dipped in cold water, then boil without stirring until the mixture becomes a medium golden color. Off heat, immediately add the butter and stir until it is melted. Combine the cream and vanilla then stir in all at once. If some of the cream lumps up don't worry. Return to medium high heat and bring to a boil. Boil to 230 degrees on a candy thermometer. Pour into a bowl. Do not stir at this point as it can become granular if you do. Allow it to come to room temperature. Refrigerate for longer storage.

Yield: 3/4 cup

Chocolate Caramel Truffle Tart

(go to www.theardentcook.com for how to photographs)

I can't begin to imagine the number of these tarts we sold over the years. A perennial favorite both for its taste and stunning basketweave finish which is so, so easy.

1 9" Chocolate Graham Cracker Crumb Crust

1 recipe caramel
Base recipe for 9" chocolate truffle tart

Microwave caramel briefly to soften if made ahead. Spread on the bottom of the crust. Set aside.

Using a rubber spatula, go around all the bottom edges of the pan in which the chocolate truffle mixture was made to insure all of the chocolate is incorporated. Pour half of the chocolate truffle filling over the caramel. Carefully place plastic film directly on top of chocolate. Place in refrigerator to set up for several hours or overnight. Strain the remaining chocolate truffle filling into a bowl and place plastic film directly over the remaining half of the filling; leave at cool room temperature overnight.

Remove film from fillings. Release the tart. Fit a pastry bag with a #48 basketweave tip. If the leftover filling is too firm to press through the bag, microwave briefly to piping consistency. Be careful not to soften too much or the chocolate will not hold its design. Starting at the top of the tart, pipe straight lines from left to right about 1/2 inch apart. Turn the tart 90 degrees (1/4 turn) and, again, starting at the top pipe another set of straight lines left to right 1/2 inch apart. Lastly, turn another 90 degrees

(1/4 turn) and pipe the last set of lines as before. You will now have the basketweave design. Finish the edge where the chocolate meets the crust with a simple reverse border (*see the finished photo*).

Place in the cooler to firm up briefly; release and cut into 10 to 12 servings. Store in the refrigerator; but serve at room temperature. This can be made several days ahead as long as it is protected from odors in the refrigerator or it freezes well. If frozen, thaw in refrigerator before bringing to room temperature to serve.

Chocolate Chip Truffle Tart

A combination of everyone's favorite, the chocolate chip cookie and indulgent chocolate truffle filling makes this more of a good thing. The tiny truffle is sure to please.

Crust

5 tablespoons butter (70 grams or 2 1/2 ounces) softened
1/4 cup brown sugar (50 grams or 1 3/4 ounce)
1/4 cup granulated sugar (50 grams or 1 3/4 ounce)
1 egg
1/2 teaspoon vanilla
3/4 cup + 1 tablespoon flour (114 grams or 4 ounces)
1/2 teaspoon baking soda
1/4 teaspoon salt
1/4 teaspoon cinnamon
1/2 cup mini semisweet chocolate chips (85 grams or 3 ounces)

Spray the sides and bottom of a 9x1 3/4 inch tart pan with removable bottom. Set aside. Preheat the oven to 350 degrees.

Cream the butter and both sugars together until light. Add the egg and vanilla and continue mixing until fluffy. In the meantime, combine the dry ingredients and whisk to mix. Add the dry ingredients, mixing well and lastly the chips. If the dough is very soft, refrigerate to firm up so it is easier to press in. Press into the bottom only of the prepared pan. Bake for 13 to 17 minutes until it is set and lightly browned. When it comes out it will be puffy and extend up the sides. Cool 5 minutes and with a spoon, press the sides of the crusts even with the rest of the tart so the crust is flat on the bottom only. Cool completely.

Filling

1 cup + 2 tablespoons 40% cream
6 tablespoons butter (85 gram or 3 ounces)
1/2 cup +1 tablespoon sugar (60 grams or 2 ounces)
11 1/2 ounces semisweet chocolate (325 grams)
1 1/4 teaspoon vanilla

Heat the cream, butter and sugar together just until the cream is steaming, the butter is melted and the sugar dissolved. Remove from the heat and submerge the chocolate under the cream. Let sit for 5 minutes. Stir to melt chocolate, changing to a whisk to smooth out completely. Whisk in vanilla. Remove 1/2 cup and refrigerate. Pour the remainder over the chocolate chip base and refrigerate. Release the tart.

Finish

1/2 cup 40 % cream
1 tablespoon powdered sugar
1/ 2 teaspoon vanilla

Whip the cream, powdered sugar and vanilla until stiff. Pipe 10 rosettes around the edge of the tart. Scoop 10 small truffles with a #100 disher or scoop, rolling them into smooth truffles and place on top of the rosettes, pressing down slightly.

Serves 10.

Chocolate Mint Truffle Tart

(go to www.europeantarts.com for how to photographs)

9" Chocolate Graham Cracker Crumb Crust
1 cup + 2 tablespoons 40% cream
6 tablespoons butter (85 grams or 3 ounces)
1/2 cup + 1 tablespoon sugar (60 grams or 2 ounces)
11 1/2 ounces (330 grams) semisweet chocolate
1 1/4 teaspoon peppermint extract
1 to 1 1/4 cups crushed peppermint candies, optional

Heat the cream, butter and sugar until the butter has melted, the sugar is dissolved and the cream is steaming but not boiling. Remove from the heat and add the chocolate submerging it below the cream. Let sit for 4 or 5 minutes. Stir the chocolate into the cream, using a whisk toward the end to smooth completely. Add the extract; stirring well. Pour all but 1/3 cup into the shell. Refrigerate to set up. Cover the remainder directly with film and store at room temperature.

Release the tart. Fit a pastry bag with a 1B tip and pipe a reverse shell on the seam between the filling and the crust. Refrigerate until about an hour before serving.

Cut into 10 to 12 servings.

Alternate Finish: A beautiful finish for this tart is to cover the inside the reverse shell with crushed peppermint candies. I used starlight mint candies that are individually wrapped. Crush about 35 mints in their wraps to keep them contained so they won't fly all over the room. Sift them to remove any powdery candy and sprinkle the remaining pieces evenly to cover the top of the tart. You will need 1 to 1 1/4 cup to cover the top.

Chocolate Truffle Tart With Candied Cranberries

(go to www.europeantarts.com, for how to photographs)

This unusual tart is perfect for the winter holidays. The cranberries, which sparkle like jewels, sit atop the truffle filling. The tart, without the candied cranberry top, can be made ahead and even frozen for longer storage. Thaw in refrigerator before assembly. The Candied Cranberries can be prepared a week ahead if desired. Top the tart with the cranberries several hours before serving.

Candied Cranberries, recipe below

9" Chocolate Crumb Crust
Base filling for Chocolate Truffle Tart

Candied Cranberries

12 ounce bag of fresh cranberries
1/2 cup water
1 3/4 cup sugar (350 grams)

Place the cranberries in a rimmed baking sheet and pick over the cranberries. Discard any that aren't plump and perfect.

Prepare a steamer by placing a rack on the bottom of a pot into which the bowl of cranberries will fit. I use an 11" wide by 3" deep braising pan with straight sides and a lid. I put a cake cooling rack on the bottom and set a 9" round cake pan with the cranberries in it on the rack. Bring the water and sugar to a full boil. Wash the sides of the pan down with cold water. Pour over the cranberries. Weight the cranberries down with a plate or two to keep them submerged below the sugar syrup. Add water to the bottom pan just below the cranberries. Cover the pan. Bring the water to a simmer and keep it at a low simmer for 15 minutes. Do not let the water boil as the berries may pop and you want to keep them as whole as possible. Cool completely.

If making these in advance, store in the refrigerator in the syrup.

Prepare the truffle filling and fill the shell to within 1/4 inch from the top. There may be a bit of filling left. Cover with plastic wrap and refrigerate to set or freeze for longer storage. If frozen, thaw in refrigerator before topping. Release from the pan. Using a slotted spoon, fill the tart with the cranberries. If the syrup is too thin to glaze the cranberries, pour it into a small saucepan, bring it to a boil and cook it to a temperature of 220 degrees. Cool completely. Spoon as much syrup over the cranberries as the tart will reasonably hold. Store in the refrigerator. Bring to room temperature before serving. Cut into 10 to 12 servings.

Chocolate Strawberry Truffle Tart, page 59

Chocolate Strawberry Truffle Tart

(go to www.europeantarts.com for how to photographs)

This is a stunning tart and what is better than chocolate-coated strawberries? To make this even more inviting, it is one of the easiest of desserts to make. It's all in the finish!

9" Chocolate Graham Cracker Crumb Crust

Base Recipe for 9" Chocolate Truffle Tart

1 quart ripe strawberries

Prepare the base recipe for the truffle tart and fill the shell. Refrigerate until set. Release from the pan. This can be done several days ahead if desired.

Several hours before serving, cut the tops off the strawberries. Place them, cut side down, on a cutting board. Depending upon the size of the strawberries, cut straight down into 4 to 6 evenly spaced slices. Keep them together and continue in this fashion with the remaining strawberries. Starting at the outer edge of the tart, lay the strawberries down slightly over the edge of the filling with the pointed ends toward the edge of the tart. Continue until you have completed the circle. Alternate a second circle of strawberries inside the first circle with the pointed ends between those of the row above. Continue in this manner until you have reached the center and completely filled the tart. The size of the circles will decrease until you have room for only about 2 to 4 slices in the middle.

Refrigerate until about 1 hour prior to serving.

Make sure to display it for several hours for maximum effect. Cut into 10 to 12 pieces.

Note: It is most helpful to have the same sized strawberries. Very, very large or really small ones should be avoided if possible. If they are of mixed sizes, try to complete the circles with the same size, starting with the largest on the outside layers and working toward the center in decreasing size.

Chocolate Raspberry Truffle Tart (cover photo)

Substitute about 18 ounces (540 grams) of firm raspberries for the strawberries.

Tropical Truffle Tart

Toasted macadamia nuts with toasted coconut and rum take to you the tropics in no time at all. This recipe calls for cream of coconut. There are several brand names - we use Coco Lopez because it is readily available in our area. Coconut cream separates in the can, so when you open it there is usually a solid white mass on top and a heavy liquid on the bottom. Empty it all into a bowl and whisk together before measuring. Do not use coconut milk – this is a different product.

9" Plain Graham Cracker Crumb Crust
1/2 cup macadamia nuts (60 grams, 2 ounces)
1 cup coconut, divided (85 grams, 3 ounces)
1/4 cup 40% cream
1/2 cup cream of coconut
10 ounces white chocolate (285 grams)
1 tablespoon dark rum
1 teaspoon vanilla

Preheat oven to 350 degrees. Place the nuts on a baking sheet and toast for about10 to 12 minutes, stirring several times, until golden brown. Cool completely; chop coarsely. Keep the oven on.

Place the coconut on a baking sheet in a single layer. Toast for about 5 minutes, stir well and continue toasting for 3 to 4 minutes. Continue toasting and stirring several minutes at a time to obtain a uniform golden brown. Cool completely.

In a double boiler combine the cream, cream of coconut and chocolate. Heat over barely simmering water, stirring often until the chocolate is melted. Whisk in the rum and vanilla. Stir in the nuts and 1/3 cup of the toasted coconut.

Pour in the shell and immediately top with the remaining coconut; pressing in lightly. Chill to set. Release and cut into 10 to 12 servings.

Bottom, Cranberry Linzer Tart, page 68
Top, Peanut Butter Mousse Tart, page 74

Nut Tarts

For all the nuts
out there!

Nut Tarts

General Notes On Nuts

Oh nuts! How often have you heard that? I can't figure that out – nuts are so good. They can be used in any segment of food during the day, eaten raw or dry or oil roasted, salted, flavored, blanched or unblanched, smoked, candied, whole, halved, chopped or minced. In addition they come with shells or without. Nuts are actually dry fruits that, for the most part, are the kernel enclosed in a shell that can be hard, medium-hard, thin and brittle or woody and tough. The popular peanut is not really a nut but a legume and Brazil nuts, botanically speaking, are seeds. But the almonds, walnuts, and macadamias used here are true nuts.

If you are buying nuts in their shells (although I don't know why you would for baking) choose those heavy for their size that do not rattle in their shells and have no cracks or holes in the shells. You will need to buy about twice as much as you will need as about half will be lost after shelling. On the other hand, if you buy shelled nuts (which I highly encourage you to do – remember, I'm trying to make this easy) try to do so where there is a fast turnover or where the nuts have been held under refrigeration or frozen. I bought a variety of shelled nuts, in different cuts from Nida Trading Co. in Illinois after I checked on how they were stored. Nuts are full of oil and can go rancid if not held under the right conditions. After buying I freeze my nuts to make sure they don't go rancid, which will ruin any dish you are making.

Another thing I almost always do is toast nuts to bring out their flavor. Toasting gives a huge boost to anything they are in and is easily done by spreading the nuts or nut pieces in a single layer on a rimmed baking sheet and popping into a preheated 350-degree oven for 5 to 12 minutes or until golden and fragrant. The time depends upon the nut and the cut of the nut. When I had the bakery we would toast a 25 or 30 pound box at once, re-carton them and freeze them to use as needed. It saved a lot of time in production. For some reason, the only nut I don't toast is the walnut and I can't give you a good reason as to why not.

While nuts are high in calcium, folic acid, magnesium, potassium, vitamin E and fiber, the reason we use them is for texture and taste.

Almond Raspberry Tart

The sophisticated taste of this tart belies its ease of preparation.

11" Plain Press-In shell, partially baked
1/2 cup good quality seedless raspberry jam or preserves (130 grams or 4 1/2 ounces)
1 cup almonds, preferably whole (170 grams or 6 ounces)
4 tablespoons unsalted butter (58 grams or 2 ounces)
2 eggs
1 egg white
1/4 teaspoon salt
3/4 cup sugar (150 grams or 5 1/3 ounces)
2 tablespoons Amaretto Liqueur
1 teaspoon vanilla
3/4 teaspoon almond extract

Spread raspberry jam over partially baked crust. Set aside.

Preheat oven to 350 degrees. Place almonds on a baking sheet and bake for 7 to 10 minutes, or until deep golden brown and very fragrant, stirring once or twice. Cool. When completely cool, grind very finely in food processor fitted with a steel blade. (Do not grind while hot or warm as they are very oily and can turn into a paste.) Set aside. Leave the oven on. Melt butter; set aside. In either a mixer or processor combine the eggs, egg whites salt and sugar. Add the almonds; mix. Add the Amaretto, vanilla and almond extract; mix. Lastly blend in the butter. Pour into shell and bake for 20 to 25 minutes or until the top is golden brown. Cool. Release from the pan.

To Serve: Sprinkle with powdered sugar; cut into 10 to 12 pieces.

Cranberry Linzer Tart

(go to www.europeantarts.com for how to photographs)

One of the most famous Viennese pastries, this couldn't be easier. While the usual filling is raspberry jam, I have substituted a bright, vibrant cranberry filling that pairs wonderfully with the nuts and cinnamon in the pastry. You could use an apple filling as well. There are several ways to get the lattice top on the tart; the one we used is quick and easy. Cranberries have a huge amount of natural pectin that allows the filling to set up very firmly. This filling is great as a jam for biscuits and scones also. It lasts for weeks in the refrigerator so it can be made well in advance.

Cranberry Filling

1 bag fresh or frozen cranberries (340 grams or 12 ounces)
3 tablespoons water
1/2 cup sugar (100 grams or 3 1/2 ounces)

Place the cranberries in a jellyroll or rimmed pan and pick over them removing any that seem over the hill. Add the water to a saucepan, the sugar and the cranberries. Bring to a boil over low heat, stirring very frequently until the cranberries start supplying additional liquid as they break. Lower the heat and cook until thickened, stirring often – about 5 to 10 minutes. Cover the top directly with plastic wrap. Cool completely before using.

Linzer Pastry

5 ounces toasted almonds or hazelnuts or a combination of the two (140 grams)
1 1/2 cups flour (205 grams or 7 ounces)
3/4 teaspoon cinnamon
3/4 cup unsalted butter, refrigerated (1 1/2 sticks or 170 grams or 6 ounces)
3/4 cup sugar (150 grams or 5 1/3 ounces)
2 egg yolks

Preheat the oven to 350 degrees. Lightly spray a 9"x3/4" tart pan with a removable bottom.

Place the almonds, flour and cinnamon in the processor and process until the almonds are powdered. Cut the butter into small pieces and add to the processor. Process until the butter is indistinguishable. Add the sugar and process until mixed. Lastly add the yolks and process until a ball forms. Do not be impatient as this may take 1 to 1 1/2 minutes.

Remove 3/4 cup (200 grams or 7 ounces) and set aside. Divide the remaining piece (565 grams or 20 ounces) in half (280 grams or 10 ounces each). Set one half aside for the bottom of the crust and divide the remaining piece in half again (140 grams or 5 ounces). Roll one piece (140 grams or 5 ounces) into a rope and place it half way around the inside edge of the pan. Repeat with the second piece. Press these firmly and evenly around the edge overlapping the edges. Press the remaining piece (280 grams or 10 ounces) evenly into the bottom of the pan. Seal the edges by pressing firmly together so no line is visible. Spread the filling evenly over the crust.

Divide the 3/4 cup pastry into 10 even balls. Roll into ropes, placing 5 evenly spaced across the tart sealing the edges firmly into the crust. Place the next 5 ropes diagonally across the tart again sealing the edges together.

Place on a baking sheet and bake for 40 to 45 minutes until lightly browned. Cool completely, remove from the pan and sprinkle lightly with powdered sugar.

Note: This is definitely best made at least the day before using. If freezing do not sprinkle with powdered sugar until it is completely thawed.

Honey Almond Tart

This unusual tart is simple but delicious. It has a delicate thin candy-like shell on the sides. We used precut almonds for this, which may not be available. You can substitute slivered almonds, chopping them lightly, or whole almonds that have been chopped. The nuts may be blanched or natural. Chop by hand if necessary, as the processor pulverizes them too much and the cut is very uneven. You are looking for about a 1/3 inch dice. The nuts can be toasted before or after cutting, it makes no difference.

Shortbread Crust

1 stick unsalted butter, softened (114 grams or 4 ounces)
1/4 cup sugar (50 grams or 1 3/4 ounces)
1 1/2 cup sifted all-purpose flour (210 grams or 7 ounces)

Preheat oven to 350 degrees.

Beat the butter and sugar together until very light, almost white. Add the flour, beat just to incorporate. Spray an 11"x1" quiche pan with a removable bottom well. Press the crust into the bottom only. Bake for 15 to 20 minutes until lightly browned. Remove from oven; set aside, leave oven on.

Filling

10 ounces almonds, chopped (285 grams)
1 stick unsalted butter (114 grams or 4 ounces)
1/4 cup honey (85 grams or 3 ounces)
2 tablespoons sugar (25 grams or 1 scant ounce)
1 cup packed brown sugar (200 grams or 7 ounces)
2 tablespoons cream
1 teaspoon almond extract

Spread the nuts on a baking sheet. Toast at 350 degrees for 5 to 10 minutes depending upon the size of the nut. Stir halfway through toasting. Toast to a light brown. Cool completely. Leave oven on.

In a saucepan, combine the butter, honey, sugar and brown sugar. Bring to a boil so bubbles cover the entire surface. Remove from heat; add the cream and almond extract. Be careful the cream may splatter when it hits the hot liquid. Stir in the nuts; pour into the shell and bake for 25 minutes. Cool completely. To release place a pointed offset spatula between the edge of the crust and the pan in 8 to 10 places. The pan will slip right off. Free the bottom with a spatula.

To Serve: Cut into 10 to 12 pieces

Mocha Glazed Macadamia Caramel Tart

(go to www.europeantarts.com for how to photographs)

This is so indulgent, it is almost sinful. To make it more so - it's very easy.

1- 11" Plain Press-In shell, partially baked
10 ounces macadamia nuts (285 grams)
1 small orange
1 stick unsalted butter (114 grams or 4 ounces)
1/4 cup honey (85 grams or 3 ounces)
2 tablespoons sugar (25 grams or 1 scant ounce)
1/2 cup brown sugar (100 grams or 3 1/2 ounces)
1 tablespoon cream

Preheat oven to 350 degrees. Toast nuts for 9 to 12 minutes depending upon the size of the nut until golden brown, stirring once or twice. Remove from oven, cool. Chop coarsely and set aside.

Grate rind from orange, set aside.

Combine butter, honey, sugar, and brown sugar. Bring to a boil so bubbles cover the entire surface. Remove from the heat, add the cream and grated orange rind. Stir in the nuts and pour into the shell. Spread out quickly. Bake for 20 to 25 minutes or until the top is covered with bubbles. Cool; release from the shell.

Mocha Glaze

1 tablespoon instant coffee
1 teaspoon water
1/2 cup 40% cream

1 tablespoon clear corn syrup
7 ounces good quality milk chocolate (200 grams)

Dissolve the coffee in the water. Heat the cream with the coffee and corn syrup until steaming but do not boil. Remove from heat and add chocolate. Let sit for a few minutes; whisk to smooth. Immediately pour over tart. Spread out and refrigerate to set.

To serve: Cut into 10 to 12 servings (or more) - this is extremely rich.

Peanut Butter Mousse Tart

If ever there were a favorite flavor in the country, it would have to be peanut butter. With or without jelly, it is a hands down favorite. This light version with a caramel topping will only add to its mystique.

1 plain Press-In shell, fully baked
1/2 cup brown sugar (100 grams or 3 1/2 ounces)
3 tablespoons cream
2 tablespoons butter
3 ounces cream cheese, room temperature (85 grams)
3 ounces peanut butter
1 teaspoon vanilla
1/4 cup cream, stiffly whipped

In a saucepan combine the brown sugar, 3 tablespoons cream and butter. Heat until the sugar is dissolved and the butter is melted. Cool to room temperature. Transfer to a mixing bowl, add the cream cheese, peanut butter and vanilla and beat until smooth and light in color.

Whip the 1/4 cup cream until stiff. Fold into above mixture and spread evenly into the prebaked shell. Refrigerate to set up.

Topping

1/ 2 cup brown sugar (100 grams or 3 1/2 ounces)
5 tablespoons butter
1/4 cup water
2 tablespoons cream
1/4 cup corn syrup

1 tablespoon + 1 teaspoon cream
150 grams whole peanuts (5 1/3 ounces)

Combine the sugar, butter, water, 2 tablespoons cream and corn syrup in a medium size saucepan. Bring to a boil and cook to a temperature of 240 degrees. Remove from the heat and stir in the 1 tablespoon +1 teaspoon cream. Lastly sir in the peanuts; pour over chilled filling. Return to the refrigerator to set up.

Release from the pan and cut into 10 to 12 servings.

S'mores Tart

(go to a www.europeantarts.com for how to photographs)

A true delight for young or old, this is quickly made and quickly eaten! I have been told that s'mores don't have nuts in them. All I can say is, mine does!

Plain Graham Cracker Crumb Crust

3/4 cup whole, shelled peanuts (85 grams or 3 ounces)
2 cups mini-marshmallows (85 grams or 3 ounces)
1 cup 40% cream
12 ounces milk chocolate (340 grams)

Place the peanuts and marshmallows evenly in the crust. Set aside.

Bring the cream to a boil, submerge the chocolate, and set aside for 5 minutes.

Stir to melt the chocolate, whisking to smooth completely. Pour over the peanuts and marshmallows, which will rise to the top. Chill to set. Release. Cut into 10 to 12 servings.

Walnut Lace Tart

One of a family of nut tarts; all with subtle but distinct variations, this one features several variations of its own.

1 Plain Press-In shell, partially baked
1 stick unsalted butter (114 grams or 4 ounces)
1/4 cup honey (85 grams or 3 ounces)
2 tablespoons sugar (25 grams or 1 scant ounce)
1/2 cup brown sugar (100 grams or 3 1/2 ounces)
1 tablespoons cream
10 ounces walnut pieces* (285 grams)
2 ounces of semisweet chocolate (58 grams)

*The walnuts should not be too fine, as they will bubble out of the crust upon baking. If you are chopping walnut halves, cut one in quarters and use that as a good guide.

In a saucepan, combine the butter, honey, sugar and brown sugar. Bring to a boil so bubbles cover the entire surface. Remove from heat; add the cream. Be careful, the cream may splatter when it hits the hot liquid. Stir in the nuts, pour into the shell and bake 25 minutes. Cool completely. Release.

Melt chocolate in microwave at 1/2 power for about 1 minute. Dip a soupspoon into the melted chocolate and wave over walnut tart in a circular motion. Repeat as desired to form a lace pattern.

Cut into 10 to 12 servings. Store and serve at room temperature. This freezes well.

Walnut Raspberry Tart: Spread 1/2 cup (130 grams or 4 1/2 ounces) good quality seedless red raspberry jam or preserves on the bottom of the shell after the shell has been baked. Proceed as directed.

Chocolate Raspberry Walnut Tart: Make the Walnut Raspberry Tart. Omit the lace on top. Bring 2/3 cup 40% cream just to a boil. Remove from heat; add 2 1/ 2 ounces (70 grams) semisweet chocolate. Let sit for a few minutes; whisk smooth. Spread over top of walnut tart. Refrigerate to set chocolate.

Top, Chocolate Truffle Tart with Candied Cranberries, page 55
Bottom, Chocolate Coconut Tart, page 85

Miscellaneous Tarts

An eclectic collection
of misfits (the best kind)

Miscellaneous Tarts

Miscellaneous Tarts

This collection of recipes consists of some really good tarts that didn't find a home in any of the other categories in this book but were made at the bakery.

Chocolate Coconut Tart

(go to www.europeantarts.com for how to photographs)

If you love coconut, this one's for you. It tastes just like the famous candy bar that all of us coconut lovers adore. The marble top is easier than it looks. This recipe calls for cream of coconut. There are several brand names - we use Coco Lopez because it is readily available in our area. Coconut cream separates in the can, so when you open it there is usually a solid white mass on top and a heavy liquid on the bottom. Empty it all into a bowl and whisk together before measuring. Do not use coconut milk – this is a different product. Often the white chocolate is very thick after it is melted. To thin it out, a plain white shortening such as Crisco or cocoa butter can be used. Any cocoa butter that states 100% cocoa butter can be used. We used it at the bakery and bought it in one ounce sticks at a drugstore in the beauty department.

1 9" Chocolate Graham Cracker Crumb Crust
3/4 cup cream of coconut (210 grams or 7 1/2 ounces)
4 ounces white chocolate 130 grams)
6 tablespoons unsalted butter
1/3 cup mascarpone (85 grams or 3 ounces)
3 3/4 cups sweetened, shredded coconut (255 grams or 9 ounces)

Heat the cream of coconut and white chocolate until melted but do not boil. Add the butter and continue to heat gently until the butter has melted. Remove from the heat; whisk in the mascarpone. Add the shredded coconut then pour into the shell.

Glaze

1/4 cup 40% cream
3 tablespoons unsalted butter
2 tablespoons clear corn syrup

4 ounces semisweet chocolate, cut up finely (115 grams)
2 ounces white chocolate, cut up finely (58 grams)

Crisco or cocoa butter

Heat the cream, butter and clear corn syrup over medium heat until the butter is melted and mixture is steaming but do not boil. Remove from the heat and add the semisweet chocolate. Let sit for several minutes; whisk gently to smooth out chocolate.

Set aside.

Place the white chocolate in a microwave container and microwave about 1 1/2 to 2 minutes on half power. Stir to smooth. If the chocolate is too thick to drizzle easily, melt a tablespoon or so of shortening or cocoa butter in a microwave. Add a little at a time until the chocolate will drop from a spoon in a steady stream without clumping up.

With an offset spatula, spread the chocolate glaze to cover the coconut just to the edge of the coconut. Immediately, dip a spoon into the melted white chocolate and holding it 6 to 8 inches over the chocolate glaze, make random circles by moving the spoon in a circular motion. Before either the glaze or white chocolate start to set, use a toothpick or bamboo skewer to draw a shallow line top to bottom near the edge of the tart. Move over about an inch and draw a shallow line bottom to top; Repeat till you get to the other side. Repeat drawing lines sideways 3 or 4 times from the top of the tart to the bottom. Lastly, pick the tart up and rap it firmly on the table to smooth out the topping. Refrigerate to set top or freeze.

The sides should just drop away; if they don't, use a pointed offset spatula between the edge of the tart and the pan. Release the bottom with a straight spatula between the bottom of the tart and the pan.

To Serve: If frozen, thaw overnight in the refrigerator. This is best served room temperature in small pieces.

Chocolate Pear Tart, page 89

Chocolate Pear Tart

One of the most unusual tarts we made, this is a testament to almost anything is better with chocolate. Pears and chocolate are not a combination seen a lot but after making this tart will it be a favorite. The cookies are bought from the grocery.

Coconut Macaroon Crust

1 3/4 cup coconut macaroon cookie crumbs (about 225 grams or 8 ounces)
2 tablespoons powdered sugar
6 tablespoons butter, melted (85 grams or 3 ounces)
8 ounces semisweet chocolate (225 grams)
10 tablespoons butter (150 grams or 5 1/3 ounces)
1 tablespoon light corn syrup
1/2 teaspoon almond extract
4 small ripe pears*

Spray a 9 x 3/4 inch tart pan with a removable rim with cooking spray. Set aside.

Preheat the oven to 350 degrees.

Crush the cookies between your hands and place them in the food processor bowl fitted with a steel blade. Add the sugar and process until finely crumbed. Add the butter and pulse to moisten the crumbs. Firmly press the crumbs evenly around the sides and on the bottom of the pan. Bake for 5 to 7 minutes until lightly colored. Cool completely.

Place the chocolate, butter and corn syrup in the top of a double boiler over simmering water. Stir until melted. Add the almond extract. Spread 1/4 cup over the bottom of the crust. Cut the pears in half and using a melon baller, scoop out the core and surrounding hard area. Place the pears, cut side down, pointed end toward the center of the tart shell. Carefully spoon the remaining glaze over the pears, covering them completely. To smooth the glaze, pick the pan up and tap it on the counter several times, shaking from side to side if necessary. Set aside for about 1 hour for glaze to set.

Release and cut into 8 servings.

Notes: This can be made the morning before serving and left at room temperature. It can also be made and refrigerated the day ahead and returned to room temperature for serving. However, the glaze will not be as shiny.

*I do not peel the pears as the glaze follows the line of the pears and if the pears are peeled they are not round and smooth which is why the pears must be very ripe. Either way is fine.

Peach Frangipane Tart with Rosemary, page 93

Peach Frangipane Tart With Rosemary

This unusual tart is perfect in the summer when fresh peaches abound. However, frozen peaches can be used out of season. If using frozen peaches, thaw them first and drain well. However, it is a must to use fresh rosemary.

Plain Press-In shell, partially baked

8 ounces almond paste (225 grams)
4 tablespoons butter (58 grams or 2 ounces)
1/4 cup sugar (25 grams or 1 scant ounce)
1/8 teaspoon almond extract
1 egg yolk
2 tablespoons flour
1/2 teaspoon salt
1/2 teaspoon finely chopped fresh rosemary
1 3/4 pounds peeled and sliced peaches (800 grams or 28 ounces)

Preheat oven to 350 degrees.

Place all the ingredients but the shell and peaches in the food processor. Process to mix completely. Pour into shell. Arrange the peaches in concentric circles. Bake for 20minutes or until set. Cool Completely.

Release from pan and cut into 10 to 12 pieces.

Rum Raisin Tart

(go to www.europeatarts.com for how to photographs)

This unique tart depends upon browning the butter for its flavor. When butter is browned, the milk solids are browned giving the butter a distinct taste. Watch carefully towards the end as it goes from brown to burned very quickly.

9" Plain Press-In shell, partially baked

Topping

6 amaretti cookies (25 grams or 1 ounce)
3 tablespoons toasted almonds (25 grams or 1 ounce)
3 tablespoons packed brown sugar (35 grams or 1.33 ounces)
1/8 teaspoon salt
1 tablespoon butter, cold (15 grams or .50 ounce)

Preheat oven to 350 degrees. Line a baking sheet with parchment or foil, spray and set aside.

Place all but the butter in a processor bowl. Process until large crumbs form. Cut the butter into several pieces and add to the bowl. Process to make crumbs. Set aside.

Filling

2/3 cup raisins (preferably the moist baking version)
2 tablespoons dark rum
3 eggs

1 cup sugar (200 grams sugar or 7 ounces)
1/2 cup flour (70 grams or 2 1/2 ounces)

1 1/2 teaspoon vanilla
1 1/2 sticks butter (170 grams or 6 ounces)

If using the dry version of raisins, combine the raisins and rum in a small bowl. Cover with film and microwave briefly to heat. Set aside while making the rest of the filling.

Mix the eggs, sugar, flour and vanilla with the paddle attachment of a mixer. Set aside.

Place the butter in a small pan. Bring to a boil. Boil gently until the butter turns a medium brown. Remove from the heat and immediately whisk into the egg batter. Stir in the raisins and rum. Pour into the shell. Sprinkle with topping. Bake for 20 to 25 minutes until set.

Cool and dust with powdered sugar before serving.

Cut into 10 servings.

Triple Chocolate Tart

(go to www.europeantarts.com for how to photographs)

We made so many of these throughout the years, I couldn't begin to estimate the number. This was a favorite banquet dessert and we served hundreds of people at a time with this beautiful, delicious tart.

11" Chocolate Press-In shell
1/2 teaspoon instant coffee
1/4 cup water
2 sticks unsalted butter, cut into pieces (225 grams or 8 ounces)
3/4 cup sugar (150 grams or 5 1/3 ounces)
9 ounces semisweet chocolate (255 grams)
6 egg yolks
2 tablespoons brandy
1/2 cup 40% cream

Dissolve instant coffee in water. Combine butter, instant coffee, and sugar in a heavy saucepan. Heat until the butter is melted, and the mixture is steaming, but not boiling, stirring constantly. Remove from heat; add the chocolate and let sit for a few minutes. Whisk to smooth chocolate. Whisk in the egg yolks and lastly the brandy.

Pour 1 2 /3 cup (400 grams or 14 ounces) into the shell. Cover the remainder and refrigerate it. Refrigerate or freeze the tart briefly just to firm the filling as quickly as possible. When firm, beat the cream just to soft peaks. Do not overbeat. If the chocolate mixture is at all set, heat briefly, stirring constantly to return to a liquid state but do not let get hot. Fold the cream into the chocolate mixture. Pour over the filling in the shell. Chill or freeze to set.

Release from the pan. Microwave the reserved, refrigerated filling very briefly, just until it is a pipeable consistency. Fit a pastry bag with a #1 open star tip and fill with the chocolate filling. Pipe the chocolate to cover the seam where the crust meets the filling. Mark your tart into the number of serving pieces you desire and make a small rosette to the right side of each mark.

Store in refrigerator or freeze.

To serve: Cut into 10 or 12 servings.

Bibliography

Food Lover's Companion, Third Edition by Sharon Tyler Herbst

The Professional Pastry Chef, Second Edition by Bo Friberg. Pastry Cream

USDA Bulletin on Butter Standards

Index

3630860R00088

Printed in Great Britain
by Amazon.co.uk, Ltd.,
Marston Gate.